CUISINE du TEMPS

CUISINE du TEMPS

JACQUES REYMOND

All measurements are in imperial and US metric. For an explanation
of cooking terminology, see the Glossary at the end of the book.

This paperback edition published in 2013
First published in Australia in 2010 by
New Holland Publishers (Australia) Pty Ltd
Sydney • Auckland • London • Cape Town

www.newhollandpublishers.com

1/66 Gibbes Street Chatswood NSW 2067 Australia
218 Lake Road Northcote Auckland New Zealand
86 Edgware Road London W2 2EA United Kingdom
Wembley Square First Floor Solan Road Gardens Cape Town 8001 South Africa

National Library of Australia Cataloguing-in-Publication Data

Reymond, Jaques.
Cuisine du temps / Jaques Reymond.

9781742574226 (pbk.)

Cookery, French.
641.5944

Managing Director: Fiona Schultz
Publisher: Linda Williams
Publishing manager: Lliane Clarke
Project editor: Diane Jardine
Designer: Tania Gomes
Production manager: Olga Dementiev
Printer: Toppan Leefung Printing Limited

Photography: Sharyn Cairns Photographer
Stylist: Indianna Ford

Keep up with New Holland Publishers on Facebook
http://www.facebook.com/NewHollandPublishers

ACKNOWLEDGEMENTS

My wife Cathy has been the driving force behind me for the past 40 years: her support and love is invaluable.

To have your four children working with you brings another dimension to the working environment: Nathalie, Joanna, Edouard and Antoine are doing just that.

The staff who have always showed me a true sense of united family spirit as well as great support and respect.

The culture of South East-Asia which has influenced me and contributed so much to define my style of cooking.

The spirits, whom I call the *grands espirits,* who have helped me to define my destiny. I first met them in Brazil when I was working in the middle of Amazonas, and they have followed me since.

Judy and Bruce Matear, on a simple and profound shake of hands to have had the opportunity to establish myself in the beautiful villa hosting now Jacques Reymond Restaurant.

Sharyn Cairns, who has reflected through her photographs the dedication, passion, excitement and innovation of our cooking.

EVERY PERSON WHO LOVES HIS WORKING ENVIRONMENT WILL HAVE A STABLE FAMILY AND A HAPPY LIFE. COOKING HAS GIVEN ME THIS AND THE INVALUABLE EXPERIENCE OF ENERGY, EXCITEMENT AND SATISFACTION.

JACQUES REYMOND

FOREWORD

Jacques Reymond is a truly remarkable man. After a lifetime of relentless work dedicated to the pleasure of others, he still has the sparkling eyes and bubbling joie de vivre he had when my wife Suzanne and I met him in his native Jura so long ago. He had already made plans to migrate to Australia, and we implored him and wife Kathy not to change their minds.

It is, of course, history that he did not, and began a stellar career, working first at Melbourne's Mietta's, then setting up his first restaurant before moving to his two-storey restaurant at 78 Williams Road, Windsor, in 1992, a 15-minute trip from Melbourne's CBD.

Fine dining in Australia has evolved at a hectic pace since the mid-1960s, in no small measure reflecting the growth of the multicultural society we have today. Some would say the need for change has gathered such momentum that we seek change for its own sake, not stopping to think whether newer is better, newest is best.

The consequence of this has been recycling of restaurants and constant reinventions of chefs and their cuisine. A few have risen above this: most notably, Hermann Schneider at Two Faces; the Grossi family at Grossi Florentino; and, of course, Jacques Reymond.

Which is not to say he has ossified. He has, as he says, continuously developed his cuisine with an eye to Asia (Japan as much as China), but the changes have been gradual, and his attitude remains founded on the standards set by the 3-star restaurants of France.

Indeed, everything about the ambience, the attention to detail, the service, the presentation of dishes, is exactly as you would expect from a French 3-star restaurant, the only difference being the cost is about one-third of France.

Finally, and miraculously, Jacques and Kathy have remained devoted to each other, to the restaurant, and to their four children, who are now part of the magic. It seems like yesterday they were knee-high or less, while today daughter Nathalie is the head sommelier, with knowledge of French wines imparted to her by Jacques, and built on by a deep understanding of the wines of the world.

James Halliday

INTRODUCTION

I believe that when enjoying food these key elements must be present: surprise, imagination, emotion and memory.

My philosophy is to use simple and humble ingredients and bring out their natural flavours. Most of the time, a product in its raw state is insipid and flavourless. This is where the skill of the person who is going to treat this product becomes so important.

Motivation, dedication and passion are what leads to innovation and creation in our industry and are the cornerstones of success. It is important to be researching new cooking techniques, new equipment and new approaches to food to be always challenging yourself.

For me, it is absurd that a chef who wants to make a name for himself should try to reproduce dishes reflecting the personality and creativity of one of his colleagues. If you copy you will never understand the art of creativity and never feel personal satisfaction.

There is no better feeling for me when I go home late from my last shift of the week to relax, than knowing I have achieved the thing that counts so much: creating a memorable experience for all the customers who have frequented my restaurant. When the body is tired but physically happy, the mind is clear and then you can appreciate better your family, your animals, the stars in the sky and the silence of the night. It is in this mood of peace, tranquility and appreciation for the natural environment that I get the inspiration for new ideas fr my dishes. I call this the inspiration of the 'great spirits'. For me this is the real luxury of life.

What has been the most important influence in my career as a chef and a restaurateur is the extraordinary power of family. To be surrounded by my wife, Kathy, and our four children, Nathalie, Joanna, Edouard and Antoine, is the most precious treasure I cherish. I also have enormous respect for my staff and I share everything I know with them, for me they are my second family. The spirit of working at Jacques Reymond restaurant has always been focused on family, and these two families give me so much energy and so many enjoyable moments. This is invaluable and unique in the hospitality industry.

Progress is the reason for success and it can only be achieved through mutual respect, communication and hard work.

This book also reflects my passion for Australia. It all started back in Brazil in 1976 when working in the Amazon. I encountered ingredients like ginger, lemongrass, kaffir lime leaves and chilli for the first time and I was immediately blown away. I had found the inspiration for my cuisine. Back in Europe I was frustrated that I could not find the ingredients necessary for my vision. With the tradition of classical cuisine still strong, people did not respond well to my innovation. We emigrated to Australia in 1983 so I could create my own style. I formed strong relationships with boutique suppliers because I knew they would help me get the best Australian products. I studied the culture and the markets of different communities and was drawn even further to the clarity and purity of Asian cuisine.

My style of cuisine has changed a lot over the years. It does take a long time to perfect your own cuisine, something young and talented chefs need to understand. At every dinner and lunch service, I still feel passionate about the food when I look at the way the staff put so much into creating a dish and finishing it with such care. Today I am proud and happy to be a chef with my own style of cuisine.

I would like to thank everyone who made the publication of this book possible. In particular Michael Smith, my chef, and my daughter, Nathalie. I hope this modest *ouvrage* will give you inspiration and memorable pleasure when you think of this magic word: cooking.

Jacques Reymond

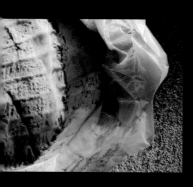

CONTENTS

Abbe

tisers

BEIGNETOFBLUE SWIMMERCRAB

1 large potato (approx 120g, 4 oz)

1 small knob ginger, julienned

100g (3½ oz) cooked Blue Swimmer Crab meat (or other fresh crabmeat)

½ birdseye chilli, deseeded and julienned

1 small shallot, finely sliced

2 tablespoons loosely packed picked coriander/cilantro

BEIGNET BATTER

50g (1²/₃ oz) plain/all purpose flour

20g (²/₃ oz) cornflour/cornstarch

20g (²/₃ oz) rice flour

1 teaspoon baking powder

100ml (3½ fl oz) soda water

50ml (1¾ fl oz) eggwhite

KAFFIR LIME EGG DRESSING

1 egg

1 teaspoon Dijon mustard

25ml (1 fl oz) lime juice

zest of 1 lime

1 kaffir lime leaf, finely sliced

160–180ml (5½–6¼ fl oz) olive oil

Simmer potato in salted water until it is cooked through; drain well removing as much water as possible. While it is still hot, crush the potato with a fork and season with salt and pepper.

Place ginger in a small pot with cold water, bring to a simmer and remove from heat. Drain and refresh in cold water. Repeat. This will take some of the sting out of the ginger. When the potato has cooled, mix one part potato with one part crab. Add ginger, chilli, shallot and coriander/cilantro to crab and potato mix. Roll crab and potato into balls approximately 2.5cm (1 in) in diameter, coat in beignet batter and deep fry.

BEIGNET BATTER

Mix dry ingredients together. Using a fork, mix soda water into dry ingredients, leaving it a little lumpy. Whisk eggwhites to a soft peak and fold into batter.

KAFFIR LIME EGG DRESSING

Place egg in a small pot of simmering water and cook for 4 minutes. Shell, then place in a small electric mixer bowl or blender. Add all other ingredients except the oil, set speed to medium. Add oil in a steady stream until a thick consistency is achieved. Serve on the side or pour over the crab beignets.

SERVES 4

GOUGÈRES

We have served gougères as an appetiser for 27 years at the restaurant. When we do something different and take them off the menu, people still request them.

250ml (8 fl oz) water

150g (5 oz) butter, cut into small knobs

pinch of nutmeg

pinch of salt

freshly ground pepper

200g (6½ oz) plain/all purpose flour

5 eggs at room temperature

120g (3¾ oz) gruyere or comte cheese, diced in ½cm (¼ in) cubes. Don't use other types of cheese or you won't get the right result. Australian gruyere is perfectly suitable for this recipe.

extra egg, beaten, for egg wash

In a large saucepan put water, butter and seasoning and bring to the boil, stirring constantly. It is very important to keep stirring so the butter mixes in with the water; that way, when you add the flour the dough forms immediately and it doesn't split.

Once boiling, turn off the heat and add the flour. Combine well and keep stirring for one minute until dough is compact and well combined. Add eggs one by one using a small mixer at a low speed, or if you do it by hand, keep the dough in the saucepan it has been cooked in. It is very important to have the dough still hot while you incorporate the eggs. Once all the eggs are incorporated, fold through the diced cheese.

Using a tablespoon, spoon onto a baking tray lined with baking paper. With a pastry brush, egg wash the tops—ensure not to let the wash drip down the sides as it will prevent them rising evenly.

Bake in a preheated fan-force oven for approximately 25 minutes at 200°C (400°F, Gas Mark 6) or 180° (350°F, Gas Mark 4)convection oven.

Take out of the oven as soon as they are cooked so they will stay crispy. Gougères can be eaten straight out of the oven or reheated as required.

This recipe is for 15–18 large gougères because once you put them on the table they will disappear in no time. You can make them any size you wish, but bigger is better.

NOTE: You can also freeze raw gougères. When ready to eat, put them straight into the hot oven, do not defrost them, and allow a few more minutes of cooking time.

MAKES 15–18 GOUGÈRES

MUDCRABIN FRAGRANT COCONUTMILK

SAMBAL PASTE

2 green chillies, deseeded and finely sliced

1 small red chilli, deseeded and finely sliced

1 clove garlic

2 teaspoons ginger, grated

15g (½ oz) palm sugar

juice of ½ lemon

½ teaspoon fish sauce (see Pantry)

2 kaffir lime leaves, finely julienned

1 shallot

2 candlenuts (see Pantry)

ASIAN SALAD

1 piece carrot, 5cm (2 in) long

1 celery stick

2 small red chillies, deseeded

¼ daikon, 5cm (2 in) long (see Pantry)

1 shallot

2 red cabbage leaves

2 spring onions (green end)

¼ bunch coriander/cilantro, picked

CRAB AND COCONUT

150ml (5¼ fl oz) coconut milk

200g (6⅔ oz) cooked crabmeat

SAMBAL PASTE

Make the sambal paste first by dry roasting the chillies in a pan. Add the chillies to a bowl with the other ingredients. Mix into a paste and puree with a stick blender.

ASIAN SALAD

Finely slice all of the ingredients except the coriander/cilantro and place in a bowl with ice water. Stand for 10 minutes, then spin in a salad spinner, add the coriander/cilantro and mix well.

CRAB AND COCONUT

In a frying pan, fry off 1 teaspoon of the sambal paste until fragrant. Deglaze with coconut milk, simmer and add the crabmeat. Heat through, making sure there is enough liquid to coat the crab. Serve the crab and coconut with the Asian salad on top as garnish.

SERVES 4

OYSTERSANDTUNA, WAKAMEANDWASABI

OYSTER DRESSING

2 teaspoons finely diced shallot

½ teaspoon finely diced garlic

2 teaspoons finely diced pickled ginger

2 teaspoons citrus ponzu (see Pantry)

2 tablespoons light soy sauce

2 tablespoons mirin (see Pantry)

2 teaspoons sake

1 teaspoon rice vinegar (see Pantry)

1 teaspoon oyster sauce

2 tablespoons soaked wakame (see Pantry)

10 thin strips of yellow fin tuna

10 oysters, freshly shucked

2 spring onions, sliced on an angle

10 small pieces of pickled ginger

2 shallots, sliced

1 teaspoon wasabi paste or fresh wasabi leaves if available (see Pantry)

4 teaspoons salmon or trout roe (eggs)

OYSTER DRESSING

Combine all the ingredients in a bowl.

Rehydrate wakame by soaking in cold water for 1–2 minutes. On a large plate, lay slices of tuna and place an oyster on each slice. On top of each oyster, place 2 slices of spring onion, ginger and shallot, then wrap each oyster with the tuna. On an Asian soup spoon, place the wakame, a dot of wasabi and then a tuna wrapped oyster, coat generously with dressing and top with salmon roe.

If you have the opportunity to substitute salmon roe for beluga or sevruga caviar, this dish will leave you with an unforgettable memory of simplicity and harmony.

TIP: Most of these Asian ingredients can be purchased in the Asian section of large supermarkets or from Asian grocery stores.

FOR 10 OYSTERS

STEAMED ROCK LOBSTER DUMPLING

90g (3 oz) firm silken tofu (we use Morinaga firm tofu)

60g (2 oz) fresh raw rock lobster meat, diced

60ml (2 fl oz) cream

2 eggwhites (85ml/3 fl oz)

small pinch salt

1 tablespoon broccoli flowers, raw

1 teaspoon hijiki, soaked and drained (see Pantry)

wakame, to garnish (see Pantry)

MISO INFUSION

½L (32 fl oz) dashi stock (see Basic Recipes)

35ml (1¼ fl oz) light soy sauce

40ml (1½ fl oz) mirin (see Pantry)

½ knob ginger, sliced and peeled

½ tablespoon white miso paste (see Pantry)

In a blender, puree tofu until smooth. Add the lobster and process until smooth—but not for too long. Place in a mixing bowl and add cream, eggwhites and salt and fold through. Mix through broccoli flowers and hijiki.

Using cling film to line small plastic moulds, place 45ml (1½ fl oz) of mixture in each and steam gently for 10 minutes.

These dumplings can be made a day in advance and reheated in a steamer as required. You can use prawn, scallop or very firm-flesh fish such as rockling or coral trout instead of rock lobster.

MISO INFUSION

Combine all the ingredients in a saucepan. Bring to a simmer, gently stirring. Then remove from the heat and strain through a muslin cloth.

TO SERVE

Rehydrate wakame by soaking in cold water for 1–2 minutes. Unwrap the dumplings and place in a cup or small Chinese soup bowl and pour over miso infusion. Garnish with rehydrated wakame. The dumplings are very delicate and fragile and a lot of care is needed when you unwrap and place them. The texture is really amazing and the miso infusion adds another dimension to this delicacy.

MAKES 8–10 DUMPLINGS

THAIBEEFSALAD INBETELLEAF

10 betel leaves (see Pantry)

HOT AND SOUR DRESSING

1 red shallot, finely diced

1 clove garlic, finely diced

1/3 long red chilli, deseeded and finely sliced

1/2 tablespoon oyster sauce

1/2 tablespoon tamarind pulp (see Pantry)

1/4 teaspoon fish sauce (see Pantry)

20ml (3/4 fl oz) ginger juice (see note)

35ml (1 1/4 fl oz) light soy sauce

25ml (1 fl oz) lime juice

100ml (3 1/2 fl oz) vegetable oil

1 teaspoon caster sugar

SALAD

180g (6 oz) beef fillet, finely sliced

1 birdseye chilli, deseeded and julienned

1 medium shallot, finely sliced

1/2 stick lemongrass, finely sliced (use only soft centre part of the lemongrass)

1 kaffir lime leaf, finely sliced (see Pantry)

1 small handful of mint and coriander/cilantro, roughly torn

1 knob ginger, finely sliced and blanched

GARNISH

1/2 teaspoon blanched and sliced ginger

1 teaspoon chopped fresh mint

1 teaspoon chopped fresh coriander/cilantro

HOT AND SOUR DRESSING

Mix all the dressing ingredients together in a large bowl and set aside.

NOTE: To make ginger juice, grate ginger on a fine grater and press holding over a bowl. Then pass the juices through a fine sieve.

SALAD

Place the beef in the hot and sour dressing to marinate for minute, but no longer. Drain.

Combine beef with salad ingredients, leaving some ginger aside for garnish. Divide into 8 portions and place on the betel leaves.

GARNISH

Mix the garnish ingredients together in a bowl and place on top of the dish. An optional garnish is roasted peanuts or roasted rice powder and fried shallots.

NOTE: Betel leaves are available from Asian grocery stores.

SERVES 5

So

FRESHTOMATO BROTHWITHSAFFRON, RICOTTAFRITTER

TOMATO BROTH

1.5kg (3 lb) ripe tomatoes, each cut into 6

1 celery stick, sliced

1 leek, sliced

3 shallots, sliced

2 garlic cloves, halved

2 red birdseye chillies, halved and deseeded

2 fresh kaffir lime leaves (see Pantry)

1 knob ginger, peeled and sliced

1 stick lemongrass, crushed

400ml (16½ fl oz) water

1 teaspoon sea salt flakes

1 teaspoon sugar (or to taste)

¼ bunch coriander/cilantro

¼ bunch basil

¼ teaspoon saffron threads

RICOTTA MIXTURE

100g (3½ oz) ricotta

1 teaspoon basil, chopped

1½ teaspoons coriander/cilantro, chopped

2 teaspoons semi-dried tomatoes, cut into small cubes

salt and pepper

NOTE: The Beignet batter needs to be made an hour before being used.

BROTH

In a large saucepan, combine all ingredients except for herbs and saffron. Cook gently at a low simmer for 20 minutes. Remove from the heat, add basil and coriander/cilantro and let herbs infuse for 5 minutes. Pass through a very fine strainer and collect broth. Add saffron threads and let infuse for 5 minutes. Strain again and set aside until ready to serve.

RICOTTA MIX

In a medium bowl, mix ricotta, herbs and semi-dried tomatoes and season. Roll into balls and set aside.

BEIGNET BATTER

50g (1²/₃ oz) plain/all purpose flour
¹/₃ teaspoon baking powder
pinch of salt
1 egg
35ml (1¼ fl oz) soda water
10g (¹/₃ oz) melted butter, cooled

BEIGNET BATTER

In a bowl, mix flour, baking powder and salt. Make a well in the centre, add the egg and mix lightly. Add the soda water and gently whisk. Add the melted butter and mix.

TO SERVE

In a saucepan, heat the broth, but don't boil.

Heat a frying pan with enough cooking oil to deep fry. Dip ricotta balls in the batter and coat well using a fork. Add to the pan and deep fry. Remove and place on a paper towel to absorb oil.

Pour broth in the bowl and place the ricotta fritter in the center.

NOTE: The broth is also delicious served cold as a very refreshing chilled summer soup.

SERVES 4

Fresh tomato broth with saffron, ricotta fritter

FRESH

BROTH

SAFFRO

FRITTE

BABYCOSLETTUCE SOUPAND PARMESANFOAM

LETTUCE SOUP

4 baby cos lettuces

400ml (12½ fl oz) chicken or vegetable stock, heated

salt and pepper

JULIENNE VEGETABLES

3 tablespoons olive oil

½ carrot, julienned

1 celery stick, julienned

1 zucchini/courgette, julienned

½ red onion, julienned

7 snow peas/mange tout, julienned

½ red capsicum/sweet red pepper, julienned

LETTUCE SOUP

Cut the stem off the lettuce, approximately 3cm (1 in) from the core. Wash leaves in cold water and drain. Blanch the leaves in a saucepan of boiling water until tender. Refresh in a bowl of ice water and drain.

Place the leaves in a food processor with 250ml (8 fl oz) of hot chicken stock and blitz until smooth. Season lightly with salt and pepper.

JULIENNE VEGETABLES

Heat the olive oil in a frying pan on medium heat. Sweat the vegetables until they are just cooked. Remove from pan.

PARMESAN FOAM

200ml (7 fl oz) cream
1 cup grated parmesan
2 gelatin leaves

PARMESAN FOAM

In a saucepan, bring the cream to the boil. Take off the heat and allow to cool. Pour the cream into a blender, add parmesan and blitz until smooth. Add gelatin and strain through a fine sieve. Allow to cool. Once set, put into a foam gun and charge.

NOTE: If you don't have a foam gun you can whip the fresh cream to soft peaks and fold through the grated parmesan.

TO SERVE

Reheat the soup and pour 100ml (3½ fl oz) into each bowl. Place 1 tablespoon of the still-warm vegetables on top. To give the dish a real 'wow' factor, top with parmesan foam. Alternatively, you can top with a piece of shaved parmesan. Garnish with watercress shoots, cubed Lacquered Pork Belly (see Pork) or deep fried tofu dipped in tempura batter (see Basic Recipes).

NOTE: To make this dish vegetarian, replace chicken stock with vegetable stock.

SERVES 4

Baby cos lettuce soup and parmesan foam

MUSHROOMBROTH LIKEACAPPUCCINO

I created this dish at the beginning of my career, and it is probably my most iconic. It's one of the very few dishes that I put on the menu every autumn and winter when mushrooms are at their best.

500g (1 lb) button mushrooms/wild mushrooms, finely sliced

50ml (1¾ fl oz) water

½ teaspoon ground white pepper

pinch sea salt flakes

50ml (1¾ fl oz) cream and 50ml (1¾ fl oz) milk, mixed together

In a saucepan, place mushrooms, water, pepper and salt. Cover with a well-fitting lid and bring to a simmer. Turn heat down to very low and cook for 20 minutes. Strain through a sieve.

Add cream and milk mixture to 100ml (3½ fl oz) of broth. Only add as much as you need otherwise you will lose the intensity of the mushroom broth. The pepper will reduce the richness of the cream and milk.

TO SERVE

Heat the mushroom broth to 80°C (160°F) and foam using a stick blender. Pour into a cup—we like to use a coffee cup and present the soup like a cappuccino. If you have fresh black truffles add a few shavings on top.

NOTE: If you are able to get slightly older mushrooms this is best as they retain a little more moisture and will give the broth more flavour. If your mushrooms are quite moist you can lower the amount of water to compensate.

SERVES 4

PEKINGDUCK CONSOMMÉ

Don't be intimidated by the long list of ingredients, this consommé does not take long to make at all and the result is well worth it. Your guests will come back for more!

½ small leek, sliced

1 celery stick, sliced

½ small fresh beetroot, sliced

1 onion, skin on, halved and blackened in a frying pan

3 cloves garlic, sliced

4 juniper berries

2 cloves

½ cinnamon stick

½ teaspoon caraway seeds

1 bay leaf

2 star-anise

4 cardamom pods

1½ birdseye chillies, deseeded

1 knob ginger, peeled and sliced

1 lemongrass stalk

1 teaspoon coriander/cilantro seeds

1 teaspoon black pepper

5 saffron threads

50g (1²/₃ oz) dried shiitake, soaked overnight (see Pantry)

1 whole Peking duck (approx 1.8kg/4 lb), including juices

2L (64 fl oz) chicken stock or water

2 tablespoons light soy sauce

1 teaspoon tamarind pulp (see Pantry)

salt and pepper

¼ bunch coriander/cilantro, washed

¼ bunch basil, washed

In a stockpot large enough to fit the duck, place all vegetables (except the shiitake mushrooms) and spices. Layer over the shiitake mushrooms and arrange the duck on top so that it will be easy to remove once it is cooked. Then pour in the chicken stock, soy sauce and tamarind pulp.

Put the pot on the stove, bring to a very light simmer and cook for 1 hour. Remove from the heat, add the coriander/cilantro and basil and steep for 5 minutes. Cool in the pot to approximately 40°C (80°F), this will take around 20 mintues.

When cooled, remove the duck being careful not to disturb the ingredients at the bottom of the stockpot. Remove the meat and set aside.

Pass the stock through a fine sieve, then pass through a muslin cloth. Pour into a bowl, cover and keep in the fridge until required. Discard the vegetables but keep the shiitake mushrooms.

Meanwhile, make the duck balls.

DUCK BALLS

1 lemongrass stalk, sliced

1 shallot, sliced

1 chilli, sliced

½ garlic clove, sliced

¼ bunch coriander/cilantro, leaves only

palm sugar, to taste

Peking duck meat

dash of fish sauce (see Pantry)

salt to taste

6 shiitake, sliced (see Pantry)

¼ winter melon (see Pantry), cut into
   small cubes

3 spring onions, sliced

Place lemongrass, shallot, chilli, garlic, coriander/cilantro and sugar into a mortar and pestle and grind into a paste. In a food processor, blitz the duck meat with 3 teaspoons of the paste. Season with a small amount of fish sauce and salt. Remove from processor and roll into balls about 2cm (³/4 in) in diameter. Refrigerate until ready to serve.

TO SERVE

Lightly and evenly coat the duck balls with tempura batter (see Basic Recipes) and deep fry. Place two duck balls in each bowl and ladle over consommé. Add shiitake mushrooms, winter melon and spring onion.

NOTE: Because the flavours are very intense and delicate, I recommend serving the consommé in an Asian-style cup to enhance their depth.

SERVES 8–10

Peking duck consommé

PEKING DUCK CONS

SEAFOOD AND SPINACH SOUP WITH COCONUT MILK

A seafood soup with curry spices and a bright green colour inspired by the traditional RouRou soup of Fiji. The Fijians use belle leaves instead of spinach and lobster meat instead of prawns. If you have fresh coconut milk, don't use water.

2 tablespoons palm oil

½ teaspoon cumin seed

½ teaspoon caraway

½ teaspoon coriander/cilantro seed

1 teaspoon brown mustard seeds

¼ teaspoon crushed white pepper

6 curry leaves

½ onion, finely sliced

4 garlic cloves, crushed

½ teaspoon grated fresh turmeric

1 tablespoon thin slices of ginger

2 birdseye chillies, deseeded

1 tablespoon kaffir lime leaves, shredded (see Pantry)

2 blue swimmer crabs, cut into pieces (approximately 100g crabmeat)

200g (6½ oz) firm-fleshed white fish

100g (3½ oz) prawn meat

300ml (10½ fl oz) coconut milk, reserve some for garnish

2 tablespoons lime juice

½ bunch coriander/cilantro leaves, boiled and pureed

1 bunch English spinach, cooked and pureed

In a large saucepan, heat oil. Add cumin, caraway, coriander/cilantro, mustard seeds, white pepper and curry leaves and fry until fragrant. Add onion, garlic, turmeric, ginger, chilli, kaffir lime leaves and seafood. Season and toss thoroughly until well combined. Add water to just cover and cook on high heat for 5 minutes.

Remove the crab meat from shells. Process the meat in a food processor. Pass through a coarse sieve and add back to the saucepan. Add the coconut milk, lime juice, puree of coriander and spinach and bring to just simmering. Remove from the stove. Pass through a medium-sized sieve. Blend well with a stick blender. Pour into bowls and drizzle with fresh coconut milk and palm oil before serving.

NOTE: If you cannot get palm oil, infuse 50ml (1¾ fl oz) of extra virgin olive oil with ½ teaspoon fresh grated turmeric. Strain out turmeric when ready to use.

SERVES 6

ZUCCHINISOUPWITH COCONUTMILKAND CORIANDER

A simple, satisfying and quick soup.

1 tablespoon olive oil

2 garlic cloves, crushed

1 small red chilli, deseeded

½ onion, sliced

1 leek, white stem only

4 zucchinis/courgettes, sliced

salt and pepper

800ml (33¾ fl oz) vegetable stock, boiling

1 bouquet garni of coriander/cilantro stems

100ml (3½ fl oz) coconut milk, frothed with stick blender

1 small handful of coriander leaves

In a wide pan, heat oil. Add the garlic, chilli and onion and sweat for 2–3 minutes. Add leek and zucchini/courgette and sweat for 10 minutes more, stirring occasionally, until the vegetables are almost cooked.

Season and add half the boiling vegetable stock. Keep on a high heat as the quick cooking helps the soup to retain its colour. Cook for 5 minutes.

Add the rest of the boiling vegetable stock and the bouquet garni and cook for another 6 minutes or until the zucchini/courgette and leeks are soft. Remove from heat and rest for 5 minutes.

Remove the bouquet garni and process the soup in a blender. Pass through a coarse sieve, pressing well. Use a stick blender to smooth the texture.

Pass again through a medium sieve, making sure the soup is smooth with a full-bodied consistency and is not too thin. It should be medium-bodied.

Pour the soup into individual bowls, top with the frothy coconut milk, drizzle with palm oil and sprinkle with coriander/cilantro leaves.

SERVES 4

Seaf

BAKEDSCALLOP ANDPARMESAN SCALLOPCEVICHE

12 Hervey Bay scallops

GINGER AND OYSTER SAUCE DRESSING

1 teaspoon ginger juice

1 teaspoon lime juice

½ teaspoon rice vinegar (see Pantry)

½ teaspoon light soy sauce

2 teaspoons olive oil

1 teaspoon oyster sauce

1 teaspoon mirin (see Pantry)

ONION FONDUE

1 salad onion, finely sliced

25ml (⁷/₈ fl oz) vegetable oil

salt and pepper

PARMESAN CRUST

8 tablespoons grated parmesan

2 tablespoons panko (see Pantry)

GINGER AND OYSTER SAUCE DRESSING

Whisk all ingredients in a bowl.

ONION FONDUE

Heat a small saucepan, add half the oil and onions. Slowly cook the onions until soft so that they do not brown. Season to taste.

PARMESAN CRUST

Combine ingredients well in a bowl and set aside.

BAKED SCALLOP DRESSING

1 shallot, finely diced
1 clove garlic, finely diced
½ teaspoon light soy sauce
15ml (½ fl oz) olive oil

4 white marinated anchovies, halved
micro herbs, shiso (see Pantry) and
  coriander/cilantro

BAKED SCALLOP DRESSING

Combine ingredients and set aside.

Preheat oven to 180°C (350°F, Gas Mark 4). On a baking tray, lay 8 scallops on their shells and add a teaspoon of the dressing, then cover with parmesan mix so the scallops are well covered. Bake for 3–4 minutes, or until cooked and golden.

CEVICHE

Heat a frying pan and sear remaining 4 scallops lightly on one side only, take out and slice into 4. Drizzle with ginger and oyster sauce dressing and top with ½ a white anchovy per serve.

To serve, place 1 teaspoon of warm onion fondue in a line on one side of each plate. Top onion with ceviche and garnish with micro herbs. Place the baked scallop opposite the ceviche scallop.

NOTE: The seared scallop is called ceviche because of its citrus component.

SERVES 4

Baked scallop and parmesan, a scallop ceviche

BAKED SCALLO
PARME
SCALLO

BLACK MUSSELS SCENTED WITH CORIANDER

This is a very quick, simple dish. The sweetness of the coconut breaks up the natural saltiness of the mussels and the coriander/cilantro paste blends wonderfully with the sea flavour of the mussel liquid.

1 tablespoon olive oil

2kg (4 lb) very fresh small black mussels, cleaned of their beards and scrubbed

100ml (3½ fl oz) cream

200ml (7 fl oz) coconut cream

dill, to garnish

CORIANDER/CILANTRO PASTE

½ bunch coriander/cilantro, picked and washed

1 chilli, deseeded and sliced

2 shallots, sliced

1 garlic clove, finely sliced

1 lemongrass stalk, tender core only, sliced

1 teaspoon fresh turmeric, grated

½ teaspoon coriander/cilantro seeds, dry roasted and crushed

50g (1²/3 oz) palm sugar, grated

2 kaffir lime leaves (see Pantry), finely sliced

1 tablespoon grapeseed oil

CORIANDER/CILANTRO PASTE

Blend all the ingredients together. This can be done ahead of time, the day before if preferred.

In a wide, heatproof dish with a tight-fitting lid, heat olive oil to a high temperature.

Add mussels and stir well for 30 seconds. Cover and cook for approximately 2 minutes. As soon as they begin to open, take off the heat, strain and reserve the liquid.

In a frying pan, fry the coriander/cilantro paste in a little oil until fragrant. Add the cooking liquid from the mussels and bring to a simmer. Whisk in the cream and coconut cream.

TO SERVE

Divide the mussels between 4 bowls, pour over the broth and garnish with a little dill.

SERVES 4

FOURPEPPERAND LEMONCALAMARI, BASILANDROCKET EMULSION, MARINATEDMACKEREL

4 fillets of small Spanish mackerel, deboned and skin scored

2 medium calamari tubes, cleaned and scored very finely

flaked sea salt

½ teaspoon dried lemon zest (see method)

COURT BOUILLON

½ fennel, sliced

½ birdseye chilli, sliced

½ celery stick, sliced

1 small leek, sliced

1 garlic clove, sliced

½ carrot, sliced

½ bay leaf

BASIL AND ROCKET EMULSION

¼ teaspoon lecithin (see Pantry)

50ml (16 fl oz) Court Bouillon (see method)

100ml (3½ fl oz) extra virgin olive oil

rocket and basil, pureed (see opposite page)

NOTE: The mackerel needs to cure overnight in the mackerel marinade in the fridge, so prepare this the day before serving.

To make the dried lemon zest, peel several lemons, remove white pith and slice very finely. Dry in an oven on very low heat for a minimum of 2 hours, being careful not to let the skin colour or burn. When dried, blitz in a spice grinder.

COURT BOULLION

Fill a saucepan with 150ml (5¼ fl oz) of water, add all ingredients. Bring to the boil then turn down to just below a simmer for 20 minutes. Strain the liquid and cool.

BASIL AND ROCKET EMULSION

Using a stick blender, blitz lecithin with warm court bouillon until dissolved. Slowly add oil until thoroughly mixed. Add basil and rocket puree.

ROCKET AND BASIL PUREE

50g (1²/₃ oz) basil leaves, picked
75g (2½ oz) rocket leaves, picked
75ml (2½ fl oz) court bouillon (see Pantry)

MACKEREL MARINADE

¼ carrot, finely sliced
½ celery stick, finely sliced
¼ onion, finely sliced
½ garlic clove, crushed
1 teaspoon pickled ginger
25ml (⁷/₈ fl oz) lemon juice
50ml (1¾ fl oz) white wine
50ml (1¾ fl oz) white vinegar
20ml (¾ fl oz) light soy sauce
10ml (¹/₃ fl oz) orange juice

FOUR PEPPER

1 teaspoon Szechuan pepper (see Pantry)
1 teaspoon pink peppercorns
1 teaspoon white peppercorns
1 teaspoon black peppercorns

ROCKET AND BASIL PUREE

Blanch basil and rocket in boiling water for 10 seconds. Remove from hot water and refresh in a bowl of ice water. Squeeze out all excess liquid from the herbs and blitz in a blender. Add court bouillon slowly and continue blending for 2 minutes. Pass through drum sieve and season with salt and pepper.

MACKEREL MARINADE

Lay the sliced vegetables on the bottom of a tray and place mackerel fillets, skin side down, on top. Mix all liquids together and pour over mackerel until just covered. Sprinkle over with pickled ginger. Cover tray with cling film to seal, making sure it is airtight. Cure overnight in the fridge.

CALAMARI

Combine all peppers in a peppermill. In a frying pan, quickly cook the calamari and season well with salt, dried lemon zest and four pepper mix.

To serve, place a small amount of squid ink spaghettini (see Pasta, Squid Ink Pasta) on each plate, top with a slice of mackerel, then place calamari on top. Spoon over a tablespoon of basil and rocket emulsion.

SERVES 4

Four pepper and lemon calamari, basil and rocket emulsion, marinated mackerel

Steamed coral trout, choko and olive dumpling, lemon yogurt and apple

STEAMED CORAL TROUT, CHOKO AND OLIVE DUMPLING, LEMON YOGURT AND APPLE

4 portions coral trout, 70g (2$^1/_3$ oz) each
salt and pepper
miso powder, to serve (see method)

LEMON YOGURT

100g (3½ oz) sheep's milk yogurt, hung
  in muslin to thicken (see note)
1 teaspoon lemon juice
1 tablespoon diced apple (optional)

MISO POWDER

1 tablespoon red miso paste (see Pantry)

LEMON YOGURT

If possible, place yogurt in a square of clean muslin cloth and hang over a basin or bowl for at least 4 hours, or overnight, to thicken. In a bowl, combine yogurt with lemon juice, adjusting lemon to taste. Place in fridge to rest for about 30 minutes.

CHOKO OLIVE DUMPLING

In a saucepan, sweat the carrot, fennel, onion and garlic in the oil. Add spices to release their flavour. Add choko and cook for a few minutes. Deglaze with white wine and reduce by half. Add bouquet garni, stock, kombu and enough water to cover and lightly simmer until vegetables are tender. Allow to cool.

Once cooled, dice the chokos, fold through the olives and season with a little salt (allowing for the natural saltiness of the olives) and pepper.

Place a large teaspoon of mixture onto a wonton skin and, using a pastry brush, brush a very small amount of water onto the skin. Place another wonton on top and seal together, expelling as much air as possible which can cause the dumpling to fall apart. Blanch dumplings in a saucepan of boiling water. Remove from water and refresh in a bowl of ice water. Set aside.

CHOKO OLIVE DUMPLING

¼ carrot, peeled and diced

¼ fennel, sliced

¼ brown onion, sliced

1 garlic clove, sliced

3 tablespoons olive oil

6 coriander/cilantro seeds

2 cloves

4 black peppercorns

1 large (or 2 small) choko, peeled and quartered

100ml (3½ fl oz) white wine

small bouquet garni (see Pantry)

200ml (7 fl oz) chicken or vegetable stock

1 small piece kombu (see Pantry)

½ teaspoon black ligurean olives, finely diced

salt and pepper

wonton skins (or use agnolotti, see Pasta)

MISO POWDER

Spread white miso paste thinly on baking paper and dry slowly in a low oven until completely dry. To form a powder, blitz dried miso in spice grinder.

TO SERVE

When ready to serve, bring a saucepan of water to the boil and place a steamer on top. Season the trout and place in steamer for about 5 minutes. For the last 2 minutes, add the dumplings to the steamer.

Place the steamed dumpling in the bottom of a shallow bowl and spoon over tomato broth (if using, see note). Place the trout on top, garnish with the yogurt and diced apple (if using). Sprinkle miso powder around the plate. You can also sprinkle some black sesame seeds over the dish as well as they work well with the tomato broth.

NOTE: You can substitute fennel or artichoke for choko, but we like choko for its ability to absorb the flavours it's cooked with. By itself, choko has a very neutral flavour but a great texture that can be used raw for crunchiness, or cooked for softness.

Tomato broth goes well with this particular dish and is quite easy to prepare (see Soups).

SERVES 4

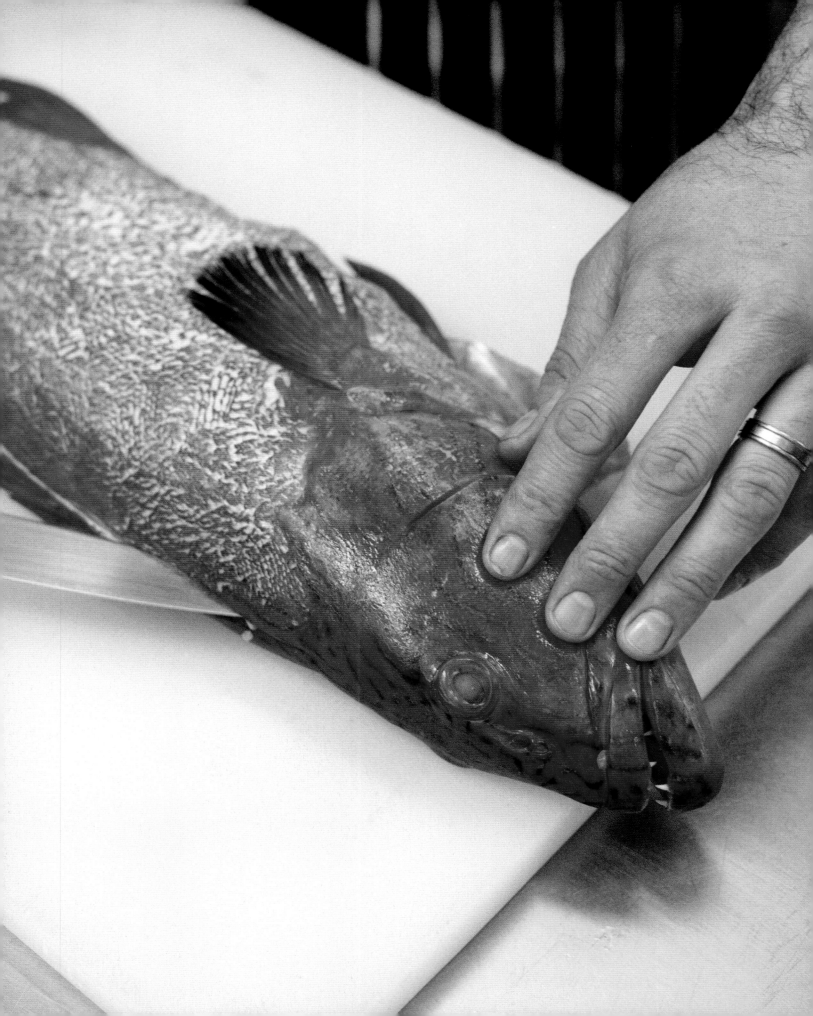

GRILLED DEBONED GARFISH AND MASCARPONE WITH LIGHT ASIAN DRESSING

4 garfish, approx 160g (5½ oz) each, deboned

3 spring onions, sliced

salt and pepper

2 tablespoons mascarpone

GARFISH DRESSING

40ml (1½ fl oz) light soy sauce

10ml (⅓ fl oz) fish sauce (see Pantry)

25ml (⅞ fl oz) mirin (see Pantry)

100ml (3½ fl oz) extra virgin olive oil

CRISPY SALAD

1 tablespoon julienned carrot

1 tablespoon julienned celery

1 tablespoon julienned daikon (see Pantry)

1 tablespoon julienned fennel

snow pea/mange tout tendrils

virgin olive oil

1 tablespoon fried garlic chips

GARFISH DRESSING

Combine all dressing ingredients and mix well.

Place garfish on a large plate, sprinkle over half of the spring onions and spoon over the dressing. Marinate for 5 minutes. Line a baking tray with foil and place garfish, skin side up, pepper and very lightly salt. Place garfish under a hot grill and cook for 20 seconds. Turn over, put a line of mascarpone into the centre of the fish and coat with marinade. Sprinkle with the reserved spring onions and place under a hot grill for 1 minute.

CRISPY SALAD

Soak carrot, celery, daikon and fennel in ice water to crisp them. Drain and dry. Mix in the snow pea tendrils.

TO SERVE

Place garfish on a serving plate and spoon over cooking juices. Dress crispy salad with pure virgin olive oil and arrange on top of garfish. Sprinkle with garlic chips.

NOTE: Mascarpone will melt like butter and gives a beautiful delicate flavour to the dish.

SERVES 4

GRILLED JUMBO GREEN PRAWNS LIKE ALA PAULISTA AS A SOUVENIR OF BRAZIL

When I worked in Sao Paulo in Brazil, I was introduced to a dish called *Camaroes a Paulista* or 'Prawns a la Paulista', which consisted of grilled prawns topped with butter, oil and garlic. My version has real fragrant flavours and is sensational when presented wrapped in a banana leaf. The bigger the prawn, the more fun and pleasure you will get making and presenting this dish.

8 large green prawns/shrimp in their shells, deveined

4 cloves garlic, finely sliced

2 large banana leaves to wrap prawns

1–2 tablespoons palm sugar, grated

1 teaspoon red miso paste, dried and ground (see Pantry)

1 tablespoon palm oil

2 birdseye chillies, julienned

1 tablespoon ginger, julienned

2 large shallots, finely sliced

4 spring onions, finely sliced

1–2 tablespoons light soy sauce

2 limes, juiced

2 tablespoons coriander/cilantro leaves, picked

steamed rice, to serve

2 limes, cut into wedges, to serve

Insert slices of garlic along prawns, they will stick out slightly. Cook prawns under a medium-hot grill for 2 minutes on each side. You want the prawns and garlic to colour evenly, so don't have the grill too hot. There is no need to add salt, as there is enough naturally in the shells as well as in the dried miso.

Preheat oven to 180°C (350°F, Gas Mark 4). Blanch the ginger slices. Place the prawns on a lightly oiled banana leaf and sprinkle with palm sugar, miso, palm oil (see note below), chilli, ginger, shallots and half the spring onions. Wrap and secure with a toothpick if necessary. Place on a baking tray and bake for 10 minutes.

Transfer the banana leaf parcel to a serving dish and bring to the table. Open the parcel, drizzle prawns with soy sauce and lime juice, sprinkle over coriander/cilantro and remaining spring onions. Add a few more drops of palm oil.

Serve with a side of steamed rice and lime wedges.

NOTE: If you can't get palm oil, infuse 50ml (1¾ fl oz) of grapeseed oil with ¼ teaspoon sesame oil and 1 teaspoon fresh turmeric.

Fresh banana leaves can be purchased from Asian grocers.

SERVES 4

QUICKFISHCURRY

One day on Turtle Island in Fiji, a guest returned from our daily deep-sea fishing trip with one of the biggest coral trout I've seen. It was lunchtime and he wanted to eat his fish immediately, with a hint of local inspiration. I asked one of my Fijian chefs to make me some fresh coconut milk (also known as a 'lolo') and we put this dish together in a few minutes, using the produce from our garden. The guest liked it so much, he ordered this dish regularly for the rest of his stay.

4 fillets white firm-fleshed fish such as snapper, rockling, harpuka, barramundi or coral trout.

250ml (8 fl oz) coconut milk

1 teaspoon grated ginger

1 chilli, sliced

few Thai basil and coriander/cilantro leaves

2 kaffir lime leaves (see Pantry)

zest and juice of 1 lime

1 teaspoon palm oil or ¼ teaspoon fresh grated turmeric

2 lemongrass stalks, crushed

salt and pepper

steamed rice, to serve

2 limes, cut in wedges, to serve

Preheat oven to 200°C (400°F, Gas Mark 6). Place the fish in a deep round ovenproof dish with a lid. Pour coconut milk over the fish and sprinkle with ginger, chilli, herbs, kaffir lime leaves, lime zest and juice over the top. Pour the palm oil all over and place lemongrass on top.

Cover with lid or a sheet of foil and cook for 10 minutes.

Serve with steamed rice and lime wedges.

SERVES 4

JOHN DORY WITH PESTO RISOTTO, MEDITERRANEAN VINAIGRETTE

8 orange segments

½ fennel, finely sliced

4 John Dory fillets, skinned, 100g (3½ oz) each

1 tablespoon light soy sauce

1 tablespoon white wine

2 tablespoons extra virgin olive oil

salt and pepper

PESTO

2 garlic cloves

dash olive oil

handful basil leaves

1 tablespoon toasted pine nuts

2 tablespoons parmesan cheese

salt and pepper, to taste

PESTO

Gently cook garlic cloves in olive oil. Allow to cool. Add to food processor and blitz with rest of pesto ingredients to form a paste, adding oil as required. Set aside.

RISOTTO

In a saucepan, heat the chicken stock. In a separate saucepan, sweat the shallots and garlic in olive oil, making sure not to colour them. Add the rice and warm through. Add the wine and reduce by half. Add the chicken stock slowly, stirring, until the rice is al dente. Add pesto to your taste, as well as a little parmesan, and season with salt and pepper to taste.

Lastly add the whipped cream. This will make the risotto light and creamy and ensure the grains don't stick together.

RISOTTO

300ml (10½ fl oz) chicken stock
1 shallot, finely diced
1 garlic clove, finely diced
1 tablespoon olive oil
200g (8 oz) aborio rice
2 tablespoon white wine
1 tablespoon parmesan cheese
salt and pepper
1 teaspoon whipped cream

MEDITERRANEAN VINAIGRETTE

1 tablespoon light soy sauce
1 tablespoon sherry vinegar
1 tablespoon mirin (see Pantry)
1 teaspoon lemon juice
150ml (5¼ fl oz) extra virgin olive oil
1 tablespoon diced tomato, flesh only
½ tablespoon currants
½ tablespoon chives
½ tablespoon toasted pine nuts

MEDITERRANEAN VINAIGRETTE

Combine all ingredients and mix well. Set aside.

Preheat oven to 180°C (350°F, Gas Mark 4). Line a baking tray with foil. Place orange segments and fennel on tray and and put John Dory fillet on top. Spoon over soy sauce, white wine and olive oil and season. Cover with another sheet of foil to enclose the fish and crimp all sides closed. Cook in oven for 6–8 minutes.

Remove from the oven and unwrap fish at the table so everyone can enjoy the sight and delicious aroma.

To serve, spoon a serving of pesto risotto onto each plate, top with a fish fillet and drizzle over with Mediterranean vinaigrette.

SERVES 4

John Dory with pesto risotto, Mediterranean vinaigrette

JOHN D

PESTO

MEDIT

VINAIG

BLACKLASAGNEOFCRAB ANDDRAGONFRUIT

This dish makes a very refreshing entrée with an interesting combination of ingredients and flavours: fruit, seafood and pasta.

240g (12 oz) freshly cooked crabmeat

red dragon fruit (see Pantry) cut into 4 rectangles 4cm x 8cm (1½ in x 3 in)

2 fresh squid ink lasagne sheets (see Squid Ink Pasta in Pasta)

WASABI DRESSING

1 egg, simmered 4 minutes, refreshed in cold water

½ shallot, diced

1 spring onion (whites only), sliced

1 teaspoon pickled ginger

zest and juice of ½ lime

1 teaspoon Dijon mustard

1 teaspoon sour cream

½ teaspoon rice wine vinegar

1 teaspoon light soy sauce

2 teaspoons mirin (see Pantry)

160ml (5½ fl oz) vegetable stock

1 teaspoon wasabi paste (see Pantry)

NAM JIM

1 garlic clove, sliced finely

1 green chilli, sliced

2 teaspoons galangal, grated (see Pantry)

2 teaspoons palm sugar, grated

½ bunch coriander/cilantro leaves, chopped

1/3 teaspoon fish sauce (see Pantry)

1 teaspoon lime juice

50ml (1¾ fl oz) grapeseed oil

WASABI DRESSING

Crack the egg and scoop out the still-gooey interior. Place all the ingredients, except oil and wasabi, in a food processor and blitz. Add oil in a slow, steady stream to make a mayonnaise. Mix wasabi powder with a small amount of water and add to dressing to taste.

CRAB

Mix the crabmeat with 4 tablespoons of wasabi dressing and put to one side.

SQUID INK PASTA

Cut into 8 rectangles, same size as dragon fruit.

NAM JIM

Crush garlic, chilli, galangal and palm sugar in a mortar and pestle to make a uniform paste. Add the chopped coriander/cilantro and pound to a fine paste. If you are making a larger quantity, you can use a blender or food processor. Add the liquids to taste.

Place a piece of dragon fruit on the plate, top with a tablespoon of crab, a rectangle of pasta, another tablespoon of crab and another rectangle of pasta. Place a line of nam jim on the plate next to the lasange.

NOTE: If you can't get dragon fruit, substitute with watermelon.

SERVES 4

MARINATED MACKEREL WITH SWEET SALAD ONIONS

A simple but tasty dish, ideal for summer dining.

4 x 100g (3½ oz) Spanish mackerel fillets

MARINADE
1 lemongrass stalk, crushed
½ lemon, finely sliced
100ml (3½ fl oz) white wine
65ml (2¼ fl oz) white wine vinegar
1 tablespoon olive oil
¼ brown onion, finely sliced
1 small knob ginger, sliced
½ carrot, sliced
1 celery stick, sliced
¼ teaspoon crushed black pepper
½ teaspoon roasted coriander seeds

THICK SOY
1 tablespoon kecap manis (see Pantry)
3 teaspoons light soy sauce

MARINADE
Mix all ingredients together and set aside.

Place mackerel fillets in a shallow dish and pour over marinade. Cover and place in fridge to marinate for a couple of hours.

THICK SOY
Mix ingredients together and set aside.

LEMON BUTTER
Combine all ingredients well. Place in fridge to set, until required.

LEMON BUTTER

100g (3½ oz) soft butter

zest of 1 lemon

½ teaspoon garlic, very finely chopped

½ teaspoon sesame oil

SALAD ONIONS

3 small white salad onions

10 almonds, crushed and peeled

2 tablespoons almond oil

1 teaspoon pickled ginger, julienned

1 tablespoon fresh coconut, shaved

2 teaspoons lemon juice

1 spring onion, sliced finely

SALAD ONIONS

In a saucepan, sweat salad onions and crushed almonds in almond oil until half cooked. Add ginger and coconut and cook for another minute. Add lemon juice and spring onion.

Remove mackerel from marinade and place on a baking tray. Coat with the thick soy sauce and place knobs of thick lemon butter on top. Grill until tender.

To serve, place mackerel on plate and serve with onions as an accompaniment.

SERVES 4

Marinated mackerel with sweet salad onions

MARIN
MACKE
WITH S
SALAD

MOOLOOLABA PRAWNS, RIGATONI WITHASAUTERNES ANDVANILLASAUCE

The inspiration for this dish is as an accompaniment for pasta. At the restaurant we serve it with a few rigatoni but there is nothing stopping you serving the prawns with a generous amount of pasta of your choice.

8 extra-large uncooked Mooloolaba prawns or jumbo king prawns, shelled and deveined
2 tablespoons olive oil

BEURRE FIN
150ml (5¼ fl oz) water
80g (2⅔ oz) butter, diced and chilled
1 tablespoon cream
salt and pepper
½ lemon, juiced

CELERY SALAD
1 celery stick
¼ cup yellow celery leaves (from the centre of the bunch)

RIGATONI
Lemon pasta (see Pasta)

BEURRE FIN
Bring water to the boil in a saucepan. Add butter, whisking until creamy. Season and add lemon juice to taste. Whisk in the cream. Remove from heat and set aside.

Add olive oil to a frying pan and seal prawns. Place the prawns in the warm beurre fin, return to the stove and keep just below simmering until fully cooked, approximately 2 minutes. Finishing prawns in a light beurre fin prevents them from drying out and retains their great texture. I find this the best way to cook shelled prawns.

CELERY SALAD
Using a peeler, peel off the outer layer of the celery and discard. Continue peeling strips off the celery and put these in iced water. Add the leaves. Remove from iced water and dry off.

RIGATONI
Cut lemon pasta into squares 4cm x 4cm (1½ in x 1½ in) and roll up into a rigatoni-like tube.

SAUTERNES AND VANILLA SAUCE

½ teaspoon vanilla pods

100ml (3½ fl oz) sauternes

½ cinnamon stick

½ star-anise

3 cardamom pods

¼ teaspoon coriander seeds

¼ teaspoon black peppercorn

250ml (8 fl oz) Crustacean Base (see
  Basic Recipes)

SAUTERNES AND VANILLA SAUCE

In a small saucepan, place all the ingredients, except crustacean coulis, and reduce by two thirds. Add crustacean coulis and reduce to the consistency of a light sauce.

TO SERVE

Place some sauternes and vanilla sauce in a bowl or soup plate, top with prawns and some of the beurre fin. Garnish with crunchy celery salad.

SERVES 4

Mooloolaba prawns, rigatoni with sauternes and vanilla sauce

Roasted dark skin flounder, garlic tempering and basil dressing

ROASTED DARK SKIN FLOUNDER, GARLIC TEMPERING AND BASIL DRESSING

The tempering on the flounder works in perfect harmony with the basil dressing and leek and fennel fondue.

2 x 0.8kg (26 oz) flounder, whole
100ml (3½ fl oz) olive oil
100g (3½ oz) butter, diced
5 sprigs of wild thyme
4 fresh bay leaves, washed
6 garlic cloves, roasted until soft
6 whole shallots, roasted until soft
salt flakes and pepper

LEEK AND FENNEL FONDUE

3 tablespoons olive oil
1 tablespoon butter
3 leeks, trimmed of the first 3 outer layers, finely sliced
2 fennel bulbs, finely sliced

TEMPERING

150ml (5¼ fl oz) pure virgin olive oil
1 tablespoon garlic, finely minced
½ teaspoon sea salt flakes
4 sprigs wild thyme
1 small fresh bay leaf

LEEK AND FENNEL FONDUE

In a saucepan, heat olive oil and butter, add leeks and fennel and cook until tender and translucent. Reserve.

TEMPERING

In a small saucepan, heat olive oil, garlic and sea salt flakes and cook very slowly until the garlic turns lightly blond. Add thyme and bay leaves and remove from heat, the garlic will continue to cook in stored heat. Set aside.

BASIL DRESSING

Mix the olive oil and vinegar together well. Add all other ingredients, season and stir to combine.

BASIL DRESSING

150ml (5¼ fl oz) pure olive oil

2 tablespoons balsamic vinegar

3 roma tomatoes, peeled, deseeded and diced

1 teaspoon black Spanish olives, diced

2 tablespoons red shallots or red Spanish onion, diced

¼ cup basil, coarsely diced

½ teaspoon chervil

½ teaspoon dill or fennel tips

salt and pepper

To cook fish, preheat oven to 180°C (350°F, Gas Mark 4). Line a roasting tray with foil and a sheet of baking paper to avoid the fish getting too much heat from the tray.

Clean and wash flounder. Score the flesh on both sides and place on the baking tray. Pour olive oil over fish, place butter, thyme and bay leaves on top and season. Cook in oven for 16 minutes.

To serve, fillet the flounder and place on a bed of leek and fennel fondue. Coat with tempering, then with basil dressing. Serve with parmesan gnocchi (see recipe in Pasta) and the whole roasted garlic and shallots.

NOTES: A thick fillet works best for this dish, so try to get large flounder if you can. If using fresh bay leaves, always wash them before using to remove dirt or chemicals from sprays used.

SERVES 4

CURED SALMON GRAVLAX WITH CITRUS AND DILL

CURED SALMON

1 x 1.5kg (3 lb) salmon side, deboned
3 cups flossy salt (see Pantry)
3½ cups caster sugar
½ bunch flat leaf parsley

MARINADE

extra virgin olive oil
zest of 1 lemon, dried and ground
zest of 1 orange, dried and ground
10 dill sprigs, roughly chopped
2 tablespoons olive oil
2 tablespoons 4 pepper mix (2 parts
   white peppercorns, 1 part pink
   peppercorns, 1 part Szechuan pepper,
   1 part black peppercorns, blended in a
   pepper grinder)
lemon juice

extra extra virgin olive oil
lemon juice
various condiments, to serve (see
   method)

NOTE: The salmon needs to cure in the fridge, so prepare this recipe the day before serving.

Remove all bones from the salmon, pin boning with tweezers if necessary, but keeping skin on. Combine salt and sugar and mix well. Sprinkle the cure mix onto the salmon flesh a little at a time and, using the parsley bunch, brush off the excess salt. This creates a skin between the salt layer and the delicate flesh of the salmon. Repeat this until the skin feels firm. Pour the remaining salt over the salmon and rub it evenly over the length of the fish so it is the same depth all over. Cover and leave to cure in the fridge for 12 hours or overnight. Rinse off the cure mix and pat dry.

MARINADE

Smear the salmon with a light layer of olive oil. Mix all the dry marinade ingredients together in a small bowl. Sprinkle marinade over fish and grind on fresh pepper mix. Wrap the salmon in cling film, making sure there is no air between the film and the fish, and rest in the fridge for a couple of hours.

To serve, unwrap and place the salmon on a large serving plate. Slice finely, sprinkle with extra virgin olive oil and lemon juice. Serve with condiments of your choosing, such as salmon roe, capers, white marinated anchovies, baby mushrooms in olive oil, sour cream, and pickled vegetables.

SERVES 8–10

WHOLE BABY SNAPPER BAKED WITH ORIENTAL FLAVOURS

VEGETABLES FOR BAKING

1 celery stick, sliced

½ bulb fennel, sliced

1 onion, sliced

1 leek, sliced

6 garlic cloves

3 birdseye chillies

2 lemongrass stalks

5 slices ginger

½ bunch fresh coriander/cilantro

½ bunch fresh basil

4 whole baby snapper or other firm, white-fleshed fish, cleaned and washed

4 tablespoons hijiki, rehydrated (see Pantry)

salt and pepper

100ml (3½ fl oz) pure virgin olive oil

3 tablespoons light soy sauce

50ml (1¾ fl oz) lime juice

100ml (3½ fl oz) mirin (see Pantry)

200ml (7 fl oz) white wine

basmati rice, to serve

green vegetables, to serve

Preheat the oven to 180°C (350°F, Gas Mark 4). Place the vegetables in the bottom of a baking tray and sprinkle fresh herbs on top. This will give the fish a great flavour.

Make 6 cuts in each snapper and insert the hijiki seaweed. Season and coat fish with the olive oil and soy sauce. Open the belly of the fish and place sitting upright on the vegetable and herb layer, rather than lying down on one side. Pour lime juice, mirin and white wine into the baking tray. Cook the snapper in the oven for 35 minutes.

Serve the snapper whole, standing on the plate. The cooking juices are full of flavour, so strain through a fine sieve and pour into a jug to serve on the side of the fish. Serve with basmati rice and wok-fried greens.

SERVES 4

ltry

CRISPYSKIN SPATCHCOCKWITH AVOCADOANDQUINOA

A very refreshing dish, the spatchcock has a wonderful, delicate flavour, so be careful not to overcook it.

2 x 500g (1 lb) spatchcock, halved and ribcage removed (ask your butcher to do this for you)

1 lemon

4 shiitakes, sliced (see Pantry)

2 birdseye chillies, deseeded and julienned

2 shallots, finely sliced

1 clove garlic, finely sliced

1 tablespoon ginger, julienned

2 spring onions, sliced

DEGLAZING LIQUIDS

10ml ($1/3$ fl oz) Chinese black vinegar (see Pantry)

15ml (½ fl oz) balsamic vinegar

10ml ($1/3$ fl oz) Worcestershire sauce

30ml (1 fl oz) mirin (see Pantry)

15ml (½ fl oz) light soy sauce

75ml (2½ fl oz) chicken stock

Rub the spatchcock skin with the lemon 5 minutes before you intend cooking it. Place in a frying pan, breast and leg skin-side down, and cook on low to medium heat until three quarters cooked—approximately 4–5 minutes, then turn over and cook the other side for a minute or two to complete cooking. Meanwhile, blanch the ginger slices.

Remove the bird from the pan and add the mushroom, chilli, shallots, garlic, blanched ginger and sauté for a minute or two. Add deglazing liquids and reduce until it has a thick, sauce-like consistency. Add the spring onion.

AVOCADO AND QUINOA BASE

2 tablespoons cooked quinoa (see
Pantry)

1 avocado, chopped into small dice

1½ tablespoons thick plain yogurt

1 teaspoon preserved lemons, diced

1 teaspoon finely sliced chives

salt and pepper, to taste

DAIKON AND CUCUMBER SALAD

continental cucumber, deseeded and
julienned to 5cm (2 in) lengths

daikon (see Pantry), peeled and
julienned to 5cm (2 in) lengths

AVOCADO AND QUINOA BASE

To cook the quinoa, place in a saucepan with water and bring
to the boil. Simmer for 5 minutes then strain.

Mix the avocado with the yogurt, preserved lemon and chives,
and season with the salt and pepper to taste.

Fold the quinoa into avocado mixture and set aside.

DAIKON AND CUCUMBER SALAD

Combine ingredients in a little ice water to make them crispier.
Drain. You can also add in some dried julienned lemon zest if
you like.

To serve, place a large tablespoon of the avocado and quinoa
base in the centre of the plates, top with a spatchcock leg and
breast. Pour over sauce and finish with daikon and cucumber
salad.

SERVES 4

Crispy skin spatchcock with avocado and quinoa

CRISPY
SPATCH
WITHA
ANDQU

ROASTED DUCK BREAST, BRAISED TURNIPS, AND A MANGO AND LEMON SAUCE

This dish is all about the four tastes: saltiness (duck), acidity (lemon), sourness (turnip) and sweetness (mango).

4 duck breasts, skin on
½ teaspoon flaked sea salt

LEMON SAUCE
2 tablespoons palm sugar, grated
¼ teaspoon Szechuan pepper (see Pantry)
¼ cinnamon stick
½ star-anise
3 cardamom pods
zest of ½ lemon
1 teaspoon julienned ginger
25ml (1 fl oz) sherry vinegar
250ml (8 fl oz) orange juice
1 teaspoon custard powder
juice of 1 lemon
½ teaspoon ginger juice

Clean the duck breast of excess sinew, score the skin and rub with salt. Place duck skin-side down in a heavy frying pan on low heat to render out the fat layer between the skin and the meat. It is not necessary to preheat the pan. Do not turn the breast until it has cooked three-quarters of the way through—approximately 15 minutes. Cook the other side for 30 seconds to a minute. Remove from pan and rest for approximately 5 minutes.

LEMON SAUCE

Caramelise the palm sugar in a small saucepan. Add the spices, lemon zest and ginger and cook until fragrant. Deglaze with sherry vinegar and orange juice and reduce by half to 125ml (4 fl oz).

To finish the sauce, add lemon juice and ginger juice to taste. Adjust consistency with custard powder.

BRAISED TURNIPS

2 small turnips, peeled and sliced
1 tablespoon sugar
30g (1 oz) butter
100ml (4 fl oz) chicken stock
salt and pepper, to taste
1 mango, sliced

BRAISED TURNIPS

Caramelise sugar in a frying pan until golden. Add a couple of small knobs of butter and the turnips. Once glazed lightly, add a little chicken stock and simmer gently until tender. You need just enough chicken stock so that by the time the liquid has evaporated, the turnips are cooked. Season with salt and pepper to taste.

TO SERVE

Put sliced mango in the centre of the plate and place braised turnips on top, then duck breast, skin-side up. Pour over lemon sauce. Pickled wombok (see Vegetables) is also an excellent accompaniment to this dish.

SERVES 4

Roasted duck breast (skin on), braised turnips and a lemon and mango sauce.

Masterstock squab with Szechuan glaze, lemon and coriander buckwheat

MASTERSTOCK SQUAB WITH SZECHUAN GLAZE, LEMON AND CORIANDER BUCKWHEAT

2 x 500g (1 lb) squab, cleaned and drumsticks tied to close cavity so no liquid gets inside the bird.

1L (32 fl oz) masterstock (see Basic Recipes)

SQUAB DRESSING

85ml (3 fl oz) squab juice

2 teaspoons balsamic vinegar

2 teaspoons Chinese rice wine (see Pantry)

2 tablespoons mirin (see Pantry)

3 tablespoons hazelnut oil

2 tablespoons grapeseed oil

½ teaspoon chopped garlic

1 teaspoon blanched ginger

1 teaspoon mustard seeds

¼ teaspoon cardamom seeds

SZECHUAN GLAZE

200ml (7 fl oz) honey

1 teaspoon juniper berries, chopped

½ tablespoon black peppercorns, crushed

½ tablespoon Szechuan pepper (see Pantry)

½ tablespoon cardamom pods, crushed

60ml (2 fl oz) malt vinegar

1 tablespoon light soy sauce

In a pot on the stove, bring the masterstock to 75°C (150°F). Add the squab and cook for 8 minutes. Rest in the stock for a further 10 minutes. Drain the stock and debone squab, reserving bones for dressing.

Put the squab bones in a saucepan with 250ml (8 fl oz) of masterstock and reduce to 85ml (2¾ fl oz). Strain through a fine sieve, and discard bones. This will give you a lovely squab juice, which you then mix with the remaining ingredients for the dressing.

SQUAB DRESSING

Roast mustard seeds and cardamon seeds, seperately, until fragrant. Blanch the ginger and chop finely. Mix all ingredients together.

SZECHUAN GLAZE

In a small saucepan, simmer honey, juniper berries and spices until reduced by half. Add malt vinegar and soy sauce and reduce by a quarter more. You can do this glaze a few days beforehand and refrigerate until required.

BLOOD ORANGE CONFIT

Break the orange into segments, retaining as much of the juice as possible to make the gastric. In a saucepan, caramelise the sugar. Deglaze with vinegar, then add the orange juice. Bring to a simmer and reduce to a thick consistency. Add turmeric and orange segments. Place a cartouche on top of the segments and allow to infuse while cooling.

BLOOD ORANGE CONFIT

1 blood orange

50g (1²/₃ oz) caster sugar

50g (1²/₃ oz) rice vinegar

1 pinch turmeric powder

LEMON CORIANDER/CILANTRO BUCKWHEAT

½ cup large buckwheat kernels

3 cups (750ml) water

½ cup coriander/cilantro leaves, washed and finely chopped

2 teaspoons preserved lemon, finely diced

extra virgin olive oil

salt and pepper, to taste

lemon juice

LEMON CORIANDER/CILANTRO BUCKWHEAT

Rinse the buckwheat thoroughly. In a saucepan, bring the water to boil, add the buckwheat and cook for 4 minutes, or until al dente. Rinse in cold water. Add coriander/cilantro, preserved lemon, olive oil, season with salt and pepper and add lemon juice to taste.

TO SERVE

Just before serving, place the birds, skin-side up, on a metal tray and pour over a generous amount of glaze. Then place under a grill for 2–3 minutes until you have a nice caramel glaze.

Place a spoonful of buckwheat in the centre of the plate, top with the glazed bird. Serve with blood orange confit on the side. If you like, add pan-roasted grapes and sautéed cavalo nero (see Saltbush Lamb Loin recipe in Lamb).

SERVES 4

PHEASANTINABAG WITHEMULSION ANDSPAETZLE

CHICKEN FARCIE

200g (6½ oz) boneless chicken breast, skin and sinews removed, diced

1 eggwhite

pinch paprika

salt and pepper, to taste

80ml (2¾ fl oz) cream

4 Swiss brown mushrooms, chopped into medium dice

1 tablespoon grapeseed oil

1 shallot, sliced

1 garlic clove, sliced

PHEASANT

1 pheasant (900g–1kg)

2 tablespoons parsley leaves

4 Swiss brown mushrooms, chopped into medium dice

1 teaspoon truffle juice (see Pantry)

1 tablespoon dry sherry

2 tablespoons sake

2 tablespoons port

1 tablespoon light soy sauce

2 tablespoons chicken stock

SPAETZLE

see Spaetzle recipe in Pasta

vegetable oil

CHICKEN FARCIE

Process the chicken in a food processor until a ball forms. Add the eggwhite and process until mixed in with the chicken. Season with paprika and salt and pepper to taste.

Add the cream and process until the texture is smooth and firm, being careful not to over process. Place in a stainless-steel container in the fridge.

Sweat mushrooms in a pan with a touch of grapeseed oil then add the shallot and garlic and stir well. Transfer to a colander to drain excess juice. Allow to cool.

Combine the mushroom mix and the chicken.

If you have left over farcie, wrap the mixture in cling film and roll into a sausage shape. Then wrap in foil and place in a steamer for 10 minutes. When cooked, serve on toast with a little mayonnaise. It is a delicious breakfast treat.

PREPARING THE PHEASANT

Bone the pheasant and cut in half. Discard the lower legs as they are too tough to eat, you can use them later to make stock. Take the breast portions and place parsley leaves between the skin and the breast meat. Place a tablespoon or two of chicken farcie in the centre of each half and fold the leg over the breast, making sure there is enough excess skin so it wraps over one another and encloses the farcie. This will help ensure the pheasant won't fall apart while it's cooking. Place each half pheasant in a medium freezer bag with the sherry, sake, port, soy sauce and chicken stock. Expel air from the bag and seal.

Fill saucepan large enough to hold pheasant with water and bring to the boil. Add bagged pheasant and simmer gently, with the lid on, for about 15 minutes. Remove bag from water and allow the pheasant to cool inside the bag.

SAUCE

100ml (3 fl oz) cream
drop lemon juice
clarified butter (see Pantry)

PHEASANT SAUCE

Take the juices from the bag, place in a saucepan and reduce by half. Add cream and simmer gently for 5 minutes. Blitz with a stick blender to aerate. The sauce should be light and frothy. Check the seasoning and, if desired, add a drop of lemon juice for a little tartness.

TO SERVE

Melt a little clarified butter in a frying pan and seal the pheasant until golden. Remove from pan and set aside. In another frying pan, heat vegetable oil and deep fry half of the spaetzle, keeping the rest of the pasta steamed. The fried and steamed pasta adds an interesting contrast of texture. Place spaetzle on the plate and arrange sliced pheasant over it. Pour over a generous amount of sauce. If desired, a crispy parmesan tuille is great addition to this dish (see Basic Recipes).

SERVES 4

Pheasant in a bag with spaetzle

PHEAS
BAG,W
EMULS
ANDSP

ROAST QUAIL IN PANDAN LEAVES

3 tablespoons olive oil

1 tablespoon ginger, julienned and blanched

1 chilli, deseeded and julienned

2 garlic cloves

3 shallots, sliced

100g (3½ oz) cooked pork belly, diced in small cubes (see lacquered pork belly recipe in Pork)

½ tablespoon hoisin sauce (see Pantry)

½ tablespoon light soy sauce

1 tablespoon loosely packed coriander/cilantro leaves

DRESSING

¼ teaspoon garlic, chopped

3 tablespoons light soy sauce

1 tablespoon rice wine vinegar (see Pantry)

2 tablespoons mirin (see Pantry)

60ml (2 fl oz) hazelnut oil

1 tablespoon Worcestershire sauce

2 teaspoons ginger, diced small and blanched

185ml (6½ fl oz) reduced quail juice or chicken stock

drop of sesame oil

salt and pepper, to season

4 quails, deboned

10 pandan leaves (see Pantry)

salt and pepper

4 small baby bok choy, washed

In a frying pan, heat a tablespoon of olive oil and sauté the blanched ginger, chilli, garlic and shallots. Remove from heat and place in a mixing bowl. Add the diced pork belly, hoisin and soy sauces and coriander/cilantro. Season to taste and mix gently.

DRESSING

Mix all the ingredients together and set aside.

QUAIL

Preheat oven to 180°C (350°F, Gas Mark 4). Place a spoonful of the farcie in the centre of each deboned quail and roll into a ball to completely enclose the farcie. Wrap each with a pandan leaf to keep farcie from spilling out of the quail. Secure leaves with a toothpick or small foil ribbons (see next page). Place quails on a cooking tray lined with baking paper. Cook the quail in oven for 15 minutes.

Meanwhile, in a pan heat up the remaining olive oil and stir-fry the bok choy until just wilted.

TO SERVE

Place the bok choy in the centre of each plate, top with quail and pour over dressing.

SERVES 4

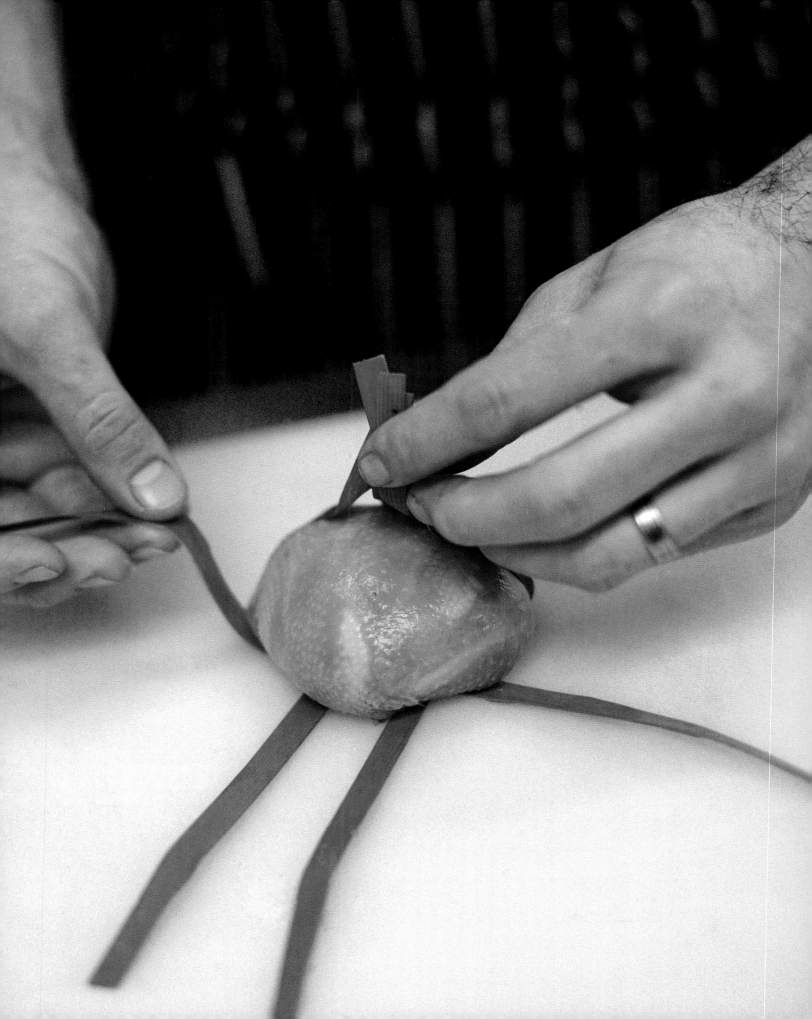

BRAISEDDUCKLEG ANDSAUCESALMIS

¼ onion, diced

⅓ carrot, diced

¼ celery stick, diced

2 thin slices of ginger

1 chilli, deseeded

2 garlic cloves, crushed

5 button mushrooms, diced

½ star-anise

6 black peppercorns

½ small cinnamon stick

3 cardamom pods

50ml (1¾ fl oz) water

50ml (1¾ fl oz) balsamic vinegar

200ml (7 fl oz) red wine

100ml (3½ fl oz) chicken stock

1 tablespoon light soy sauce

2 tablespoons mirin (see Pantry)

1 tablespoon Worcestershire sauce

3 tablespoons vegetable oil

4 duck legs

In a casserole dish large enough to fit the duck legs lying flat on the bottom, sweat vegetables in a little oil with spices until fragrant. Deglaze with water and scrape the bottom to loosen any of the natural caramelised sugars from the vegetables. Add the balsamic vinegar and reduce by half, then add the rest of the liquid ingredients and bring to a simmer.

Preheat oven to 170°C (325°F, Gas Mark 2–3). In a frying pan, heat oil and seal the duck legs until brown, place skin-side up in the casserole dish with the stock and cover with a sheet of baking paper. Place lid on top and cook in oven for 1 hour. The duck flesh should be very tender and fall away from the bone easily when cooked.

To make the sauce, remove the duck legs from the casserole dish and strain the stock, discarding the vegetables. Skim off any fat and reduce the liquid until it has a thick sauce consistency.

Serve the duck on a bed of mild spiced lentils (see Vegetables). Pour over sauce.

NOTE: This recipe is ideal for preparing a variety of braising meats, such as osso bucco, oxtail, lamb or veal shanks or beef cheeks.

SERVES 4

SPICEDFRIEDQUAIL WITHASIANDRESSING

4 jumbo quails, split in half
oil for deep frying

MARINADE

50ml (1¾ fl oz) light soy sauce

3 tablespoons grapeseed oil

1 teaspoon grated ginger

2 garlic cloves, finely diced

1 teaspoon roasted Szechuan pepper
(see Pantry)

¼ teaspoon five-spice powder

50ml (1¾ fl oz) shaoxing wine (see
Pantry)

SPICED FLOUR

½ cup plain/all purpose flour

½ teaspoon flaked salt

½ teaspoon paprika

½ teaspoon ground Szechuan pepper
(see Pantry)

½ teaspoon ground five-spice powder

¼ teaspoon ground ginger

MARINADE

Combine all ingredients together and set aside.

SPICED FLOUR

Combine all ingredients together and set aside.

Split the quails in half and place in a dish, pour over marinade, cover and place in fridge for 20 minutes. Drain then dust in spiced flour. Heat vegetable oil in a frying pan and deep fry quails until crisp. Drain the oil to use in the dressing.

ASIAN DRESSING

2 chillies, deseeded and sliced

3 spring onions, sliced

salt

1 tablespoon mirin (see Pantry)

1 tablespoon sake

50ml (1¾ fl oz) hot oil from frying quails

NOODLE SALAD

½ packet thin glass noodles

zest of 1 lemon cut into very thin
  julienne slices and blanched twice

½ tablespoon julienned ginger,
  blanched twice

2 red shallots, finely sliced

¼ red capsicum/sweet pepper, thinly
  julienned

sprigs of coriander/cilantro and
  Vietnamese mint

ASIAN DRESSING

Combine all ingredients, except oil, in a bowl. Set aside.

NOODLE SALAD

Soak the glass noodles in hot water for 5 minutes to soften. Drain. When noodles have cooled, mix together with the salad ingredients and arrange on plates. Top with fried quail. Add hot oil to the dressing, mix and pour over quail and noodle salad.

SERVES 4

Spiced fried quail with Asian dressing

Mild red curry of young pigeon and fragrant coconut milk

MILD RED CURRY OF YOUNG PIGEON AND FRAGRANT COCONUT MILK

The clean fresh Asian fragrance and flavours in this dish come alive with the coconut milk and curry paste, contrasting with the pigeon flavour to create a memorable taste sensation.

RED CURRY PASTE

1 tablespoon shrimp paste

½ teaspoon white peppercorns, dry roasted

½ teaspoon coriander/cilantro seeds, dry roasted

3 birdseye chillies, half the seeds removed

3 shallots, sliced

2 garlic cloves, sliced

½ lemongrass stalk, finely sliced

2 kaffir lime leaves (see Pantry)

½ tablespoon grated galangal (see Pantry)

1 teaspoon grated ginger

1½ tablespoons coriander/cilantro root and stem, rinsed well, chopped

few drops fish sauce

oil to blend, if necessary

RED CURRY

3 tablespoons grapeseed oil

2 young pigeons, 500g (1lb) each, split in half and wiped of any sign of blood

3 tablespoons curry paste

400ml (12½ fl oz) clear chicken stock

RED CURRY PASTE

Wrap the shrimp paste in foil and roast in the oven for 7–10 minutes.

Dry roast the dried spices in a frying pan on low heat. Combine with shrimp paste. Place all ingredients in a food processor and blitz until an even paste. Add oil if you have trouble blending together.

RED CURRY

In a frying pan, heat 2 tablespoons grapeseed oil and gently sear the pigeon skin-side down for 5 minutes, remove from pan and set aside. In the same pan, heat remaining grapeseed oil over low flame and fry paste until fragrant, approximately 5 minutes. Add chicken stock and bring to a simmer, scraping the bottom well with a wooden spoon. Place the seared pigeon in a casserole dish, skin-side up, pour over the stock and cook on the stove top at a very low simmer for 1½ hours.

FRAGRANT COCONUT MILK

400ml (12½ fl oz) coconut milk

1 small knob of galangal, peeled and sliced (see Pantry)

1 small knob of ginger, peeled and sliced

1 shallot, sliced

1 chilli, deseeded

2 kaffir lime leaves

1 lemongrass stalk, crushed

4 fresh curry leaves

¼ bunch of coriander/cilantro

¼ bunch of basil

½ lime, juiced

FRAGRANT COCONUT MILK

In a saucepan, place all ingredients except the coriander/cilantro, basil and lime juice and keep just below a simmer, approximately 75°C (150°F), for 20 minutes. Take the saucepan off the heat and add the coriander/cilantro, basil and lime juice and infuse for 5 minutes, then strain liquid and reserve.

TO SERVE

Place half a pigeon on a plate, spoon over cooking juices and drizzle with fragrant coconut milk. Serve with steamed rice. You can substitute the pigeon for duck or a small chicken, just adjust the cooking time. We use pigeon for its red dense flesh and unique flavour.

SERVES 4

TEASMOKED CHICKEN

4L (128 fl oz) masterstock (see Basic Recipes)

1 chicken, 1.8kg (3½ lb)

4 tablespoons brown crystal sugar

2 tablespoons black Chinese tea

1 tablespoon short grain rice

CUCUMBER AND POACHED SHIITAKE SALAD

½ cucumber

12 shiitake, poached

1 teaspoon black sesame seeds

Place all Masterstock ingredients in a large saucepan and cook slowly for 1 hour. Place chicken in stock and poach at 80°C (160°F) for 40 minutes, making sure that the chicken is immersed in the stock at all times and the temperature does not go over 80°C. Once the chicken is cooked, take it out of the stock and pat dry with a paper towel. Line the bottom of a large wok with 2 sheets of aluminum foil, sprinkle the sugar, tea and rice onto the foil and heat up until the sugar starts to caramelise. Place the chicken on a rack and put inside the wok. Cover tightly with a lid and smoke for 10 minutes. Remove chicken from rack.

CUCUMBER AND POACHED SHIITAKE SALAD

Combine salad ingredients.

To serve, slice chicken and serve with a cucumber and poached shiitake salad sprinkled with roasted black sesame seeds on the side.

NOTE: Chicken poached in Masterstock has an exceptional flavour and colour, which is enhanced even more by smoking over black Chinese tea. Don't smoke for more than 10 minutes or it will be too strong. After poaching the chicken, you can retain the Masterstock and freeze for another dish.

SERVES 4

Chicken poached in Masterstock

HOISINGLAZED WHITERABBIT ANDPOTATO BOULANGÈRES

HOISIN GLAZE

3 tablespoons hoisin (see Pantry)

3 tablespoons Dijon mustard

½ teaspoon light soy sauce

RABBIT SAUCE

1 x white farmed rabbit, 1.2kg–1.5kg (1²/₃ lb–3 lb), forequarter only

1 tablespoon grapeseed oil

1 small knob butter

½ carrot, cut into small dice

½ celery stick, cut into small dice

1 garlic clove, crushed

1 small knob ginger, finely sliced

2 teaspoons sugar

3 tablespoons balsamic vinegar

500ml (16 fl oz) water

1 tablespoon light soy sauce

1 tablespoon Dijon mustard

2 teaspoons hoisin sauce

½ tablespoon Worstershire sauce

Remove forequarter of the rabbit by cutting it across it the body behind its shoulders. You can ask your butcher to do this for you. Cut forequarter in half and reserve for the sauce. The other part of the rabbit is called 'the baron' and comprises the saddle, or back of the rabbit, with the back legs still attached.

HOISIN GLAZE

Mix hoisin and Dijon mustard together and add the soy sauce. Set aside until required.

RABBIT SAUCE

In a large saucepan, sear the forequarter of the rabbit lightly with a tablespoon of grapeseed oil and a knob of butter. Add carrot, celery, garlic and ginger and sweat for 5 minutes; add sugar and caramelise. Add balsamic vinegar and reduce sauce by half. Add water, soy sauce, mustard and hoisin and cook at low simmer for at least 45 minutes. Strain the sauce, return to pan and add Worcestershire sauce, mix well to combine and reduce to desired thick sauce-like consistency.

POTATO BOULANGÈRES

1 brown onion, peeled and finely sliced

3 large desiree potatoes, peeled

70g (2^1/$_3$ oz) unsalted butter, diced

pinch of paprika

salt and pepper to season

400ml (12½ fl oz) chicken stock

4 sprigs wild thyme

3 tablespoons olive oil

POTATO BOULANGÈRES

Preheat oven to 180°C (350°F, Gas Mark 4). Line a baking tray large enough to accommodate the rabbit with a sheet of baking paper smeared with butter. Slice the onion finely and spread over the paper. Slice the potatoes finely and arrange on top of the onions covering the base of the baking tray completely. Scatter the butter on top, sprinkle with paprika, season lightly with salt and pepper and add chicken stock making sure not to cover the potatoes completely. Sprinkle with wild thyme.

Coat the rabbit baron completely with the hoisin glaze and place on top of the potatoes, drizzle over with olive oil and cook in the oven for 40 minutes.

TO SERVE

Bring the whole baking tray to the table and let everyone help themselves to this humble, simple and comforting dish. Don't forget the sauce!

NOTE: Keep the cooked forequarter pieces from the sauce, they make a very tasty accompaniment for a salad the next day with a drop of good virgin olive oil on top. The shoulders have a lot of meat on them and are very moist.

SERVES 4–6

Hoisin glazed white rabbit and potato boulangères

Po

LACQUERED
PORKBELLY

½ pork belly of a young pig

60g (2 oz) soft brown sugar

75ml (2½ fl oz) Chinese black vinegar (see Pantry)

2 black peppercorns

1 cinnamon stick

2 cardamom pods

2 star-anise

1 dried chilli

2 strips orange skin

1 small knob ginger, sliced

2 cloves garlic

1 celery stick, diced

½ carrot, diced

25ml ($^7/_8$ fl oz) light soy sauce

50ml (1¾ fl oz) sake

½ tablespoon dark soy sauce

25ml ($^7/_8$ fl oz) shaoxing wine (see Pantry)

100ml (3½ fl oz) white wine

Preheat oven to 160°C (325°F, Gas Mark 2–3). With a very sharp knife, score the skin of the belly and blanch in a pot of hot water, no hotter than 75°C (165°F), for 30 seconds. Remove from the water and allow to dry for 15 minutes on a resting rack. In a heavy based pan, caramelise the sugar. Deglaze with black vinegar. Once the sugar has dissolved, add the pork belly, skin side down, and let it caramelise gently, this will take 4–5 minutes. Once caramelised, add all the dry spices, orange zest, ginger, garlic, celery and carrot and sweat for 2 minutes. Deglaze with the remaining liquids so it comes halfway up the belly, you may need to add a little water. Cover with baking paper and foil. Cook in oven for 3 hours or until tender.

SAUCE

200ml (7 fl oz) of reduced cooking juices
  from pork

1 tablespoon light soy sauce

1 tablespoon balsamic vinegar

1 tablespoon mirin

1 tablespoon Dijon mustard

KAKIAGE

Tempura batter (see Basic Recipes)

4 snow peas/mange tout, halved

4 small wedges pumpkin, peeled

4 round daikon slices (see Pantry)

4 pieces red capsicum/sweet red pepper

SAUCE

For the sauce, strain the cooking juices into a saucepan. Reduce by half. Add soy sauce, balsamic vinegar, mirin and Dijon mustard. Mix well and strain.

KAKIAGE

Thread the vegetables onto a small bamboo skewer. Coat lightly with tempura batter and deep fry. Serving the pork belly with the tempura vegetables will add a crunchiness that contrasts well with the soft texture of the meat. You can also serve it with steamed Asian greens such as baby bok choy.

The pork belly will keep refrigerated for a week and can be used for a variety of dishes, either on its own or as part of another dish, such as Baby Cos Lettuce Soup (see Soups), ravioli, stuffed meat and poultry and stuffed vegetables.

SERVES 4

Lacquered pork belly

SUCKLING PIG

Suckling pig (3kg–4kg/6 lb–8¹⁄₂ lb)
(Order from your butcher. It may take a
couple of days)

100ml (3¹⁄₂ fl oz) water

500ml (16 fl oz) chicken stock

10 cumin seeds

7 juniper berries

1 small knob fresh ginger

1 bouquet garni (see Pantry)

1 teaspoon white sesame seeds

2 teaspoons honey

2 teaspoons sea salt

6 black peppercorns

SUCKLING PIG DRESSING

100ml (3¹⁄₂ fl oz) reduced cooking liquid
from pig (see method)

100ml (3¹⁄₂ fl oz) extra virgin olive oil

25ml (⁷⁄₈ fl oz) sake

25ml (⁷⁄₈ fl oz) light soy sauce

drop of sesame oil

15ml (¹⁄₂ fl oz) Worcestershire sauce

2 shallots, small dice

¹⁄₂ small piece ginger, diced and
blanched

¹⁄₂ clove garlic, finely diced

1 tablespoon spring onion, sliced

Preheat oven to 120°C (250°F, Gas Mark 1). In a large baking tray, big enough to hold the whole pig, put water, chicken stock and spices. Sprinkle sesame seeds on the underside of the pig and place, skin-side up, in the tray. Rub skin with honey, sprinkle with salt and pepper and place in oven for 4 hours. The slow cooking and liquids in the tray will ensure the pig retains its moisture and delicate flavour. Once cooked, remove from oven (debone if preferred). To crisp the skin, turn oven up to 200°C (400°F, Gas Mark 6) and put pig back in the oven until crispy, being careful not to burn it. Reserve cooking liquids for dressing.

SUCKLING PIG DRESSING

Place the reserved cooking liquids in a saucepan on the stove and reduce. In a large bowl, combine the liquid with the rest of the ingredients and mix well. Set aside until ready to serve.

TO SERVE

Leave on the head and trotters for dramatic effect. Slice the pork thickly and serve on top of an embeurrée of savoy cabbage (see Vegetables). Pour dressing over. If you like, slice potatoes and cook in the baking tray under the suckling pig—they are the most delicious braised potatoes.

SERVES 8–10 PEOPLE

LAMBCUTLETFARCIE WITHSILVERBEET, TAMARINDAND GINGERDRESSING

I like the combination of the steely flavour of the silverbeet with the sourness and tanginess of the tamarind and the astringency of the ginger.

rock salt to cover the bottom of baking tray

120g (4 oz) chicken fillet

1 eggwhite

salt and pepper, to season

pinch of paprika

60ml (2 fl oz) cream, reserving a splash for the silverbeet

50ml (1¾ fl oz) cream

80g (2⅔ oz) sweetbreads, blanched and cleaned

60g (2 oz) button mushrooms, cut in small cubes

garlic clove, sliced

1 shallot, diced

16 double lamb cutlets—2 points (keep only one bone on each cutlet—ask your butcher to prepare for you)

8 parsley leaves

crepinette, thin and clean, very white (see Pantry)

3 tablespoons clarified butter (see Pantry)

FARCIE

Preheat oven to 180°C (350°F, Gas Mark 4). Pour rock salt into a baking tray to create a bed that covers the bottom of the tray completely and place in the oven.

Process the chicken in a food processer until a ball of chicken meat forms. Add the eggwhite and process again for 10 seconds. Season with salt, pepper and paprika. Add the cream in a slow stream and process for a few seconds until the ingredients are well mixed, scraping the sides as required. Place in a stainless steel bowl in the fridge.

Sauté sweetbreads and mushrooms until tender then add the garlic and shallot stirring quickly. Put aside to cool. Once cold, combine with the chicken mix.

Place a tablespoon of the mix on top of each cutlet. Put parsley leaves on top and wrap up in crepinette using as little crepinette as possible. In a pan, heat clarified butter and seal each side of the cutlet for about 5 seconds per side, or until golden. Remove the cutlet from the pan, place on preheated salt tray and cook in the oven for 5 minutes.

SILVERBEET

½ bunch silverbeet, stems peeled, leaves whole

1 tablespoon butter

2 tablespoons olive oil

1 tablespoon sherry vinegar

dash of cream

TAMARIND AND GINGER DRESSING

300ml (10½ fl oz) chicken stock

½ tablespoon tamarind paste

1 shallot, finely diced

1 garlic clove, finely diced

1 chilli, deseeded

½ knob ginger, sliced

1 teaspoon red miso paste (see Pantry)

¼ bunch coriander, picked

1 tablespoon light soy sauce

2 tablespoons balsamic vinegar

1 tablespoon mirin (see Pantry)

90ml (3¼ fl oz) pure virgin olive oil

1 shallot, sliced

1 garlic clove, crushed

1 tablespoon chopped chives

SILVERBEET

Blanch the silverbeet and refresh. Dice coarsely, mixing the leaves and stems and stir-fry in a wok with butter and olive oil. Season. Add a touch of sherry vinegar and a splash of cream. Remove from the wok and set aside.

TAMARIND AND GINGER DRESSING

Put stock, tamarind paste, shallot, garlic, chilli, ginger and red miso paste in a small saucepan and cook over a moderate heat until liquid is reduced by half. Add coriander and infuse for 2 minutes. Strain and place the liquid in a bowl.

Add the soy sauce, balsamic vinegar, mirin, olive oil, shallot, garlic and chives to the bowl and mix well. Set aside.

TO SERVE

In the centre of the plate, place a soup spoon of silverbeet. Arrange the cutlets on each side and coat the lamb and silverbeet with the dressing.

NOTE: Cooking the lamb on rock salt prevents it from drying out and keeps all the moisture and texture in the meat. If you are refrigerating overnight to eat the next day, this technique will also stop the meat from going grey. It's the best technique we have developed for cooking lamb.

SERVES 4

Lamb cutlet farcie with silverbeet, tamarind and ginger dressing

LAMBC

WITHS

TAMAR

GINGE

LAMB RACK WITH OYSTER SAUCE, BORLOTTI BEAN PUREE AND MINT OIL

LAMB

1 x 8 point rack of lamb (ask your butcher to French polish the bones for you)

3 tablespoons oyster sauce

½ teaspoon soy sauce

1 teaspoon white sesame seeds, lightly toasted

MINT OIL

½ bunch mint

50ml (1¾ fl oz) extra virgin olive oil

1 teaspoon mirin (see Pantry)

1 teaspoon rice wine vinegar (see Pantry)

salt and pepper

LAMB

Preheat oven to 180°C (350°F, Gas Mark 4). Pour rock salt into a baking tray to create a bed that covers the bottom of the tray completely and place in the oven.

Mix oyster and soy sauces and set aside.

Trim lamb of any excess fat and sinews. In a pan, seal lamb until golden all over.

Place lamb on tray of rock salt and cook in oven for approximately 7 minutes. The lamb should still be a little undercooked. Apply a good layer—about 3mm (¼in) thick—of oyster and soy sauce on the lamb and return to the oven for a further 3–5 minutes or until cooked to your liking. Remove from the rock salt as soon as it comes out of the oven, as it may continue cooking from any residual heat in the salt.

Allow meat to rest for at least 5 minutes then sprinkle with sesame seeds.

NOTE: French polishing lamb bones means to remove all the fat sinew and meat from the bone.

MINT OIL

Place the mint and oil into the smallest round container possible to fit a stick blender and blitz until mint is finely chopped. Add mirin, rice wine vinegar and a little salt and pepper to taste.

ASIAN SALAD

¼ carrot, julienned

¼ diakon, julienned

1 birdseye chilli, deseeded and julienned

2 spring onions, green part, sliced finely on diagonal

¼ bunch coriander leaves, picked

ASIAN SALAD

Mix all ingredients together.

TO SERVE

Place the lamb on a plate with a little Asian salad and mint oil on the side.

NOTE: If you would like a carbohydrate dish to accompany, you can include a side of borlotti beans purreed with truffle oil (see Vegetables).

The lacquered lamb not only looks stunning but its coating goes so well with the mint oil and the refreshing, crispy salad that you don't need a sauce. The oyster and soy coating are sufficient.

Cooking the lamb on rock salt prevents it from drying out and keeps all the moisture and texture in the meat. If you are refrigerating overnight to eat the next day, this technique will also stop the meat from going grey. It's the best technique we have developed for cooking lamb.

SERVES 4

Lamb rack with oyster sauce, borlotti bean puree and mint oil

LAMBR
OYSTER
BORLO
PUREE

SALTBUSHLAMBLOIN, SLOWROASTEDONION ANDCAVALONERO

2 saltbush lamb loins or regular lamb loins (280g/9½ oz each)

SLOW ROASTED ONIONS

6 medium white salad onions

rock salt

salt and pepper

3 tablespoons olive oil

1 tablespoon finely sliced chives

2 spring onions, white part only, finely sliced

LOIN MARINADE

1 shallot, sliced

3 spring onions, sliced

1 small knob ginger, peeled and sliced

1 clove garlic, skin on, crushed

1 bay leaf

3 sprigs thyme

1 tablespoon oyster sauce

80ml (2¾ fl oz) soy sauce

200ml (7 fl oz) olive oil

CAVALO NERO

2 tablespoons extra virgin olive oil

4 small lamb merguez sausages, sliced

8 cavalo nero leaves (see Pantry)

1 tablespoon garlic chips

8 small orange segments

SLOW ROASTED ONIONS

Preheat oven to 140°C (300°F, Gas Mark 2). Place the onions on a tray lined with a thin layer of rock salt and bake until very soft and sweet—about two hours. Cool a little, then peel the outer layer off and discard. Peel onions further into small strips. Place in a small bowl, season and add olive oil, chives and spring onions. This cooking technique gives these onions so much taste they don't need many condiments.

LOIN MARINADE

Combine the marinade ingredients in a small bowl. Divide the marinade in half into two larger bowls.

Clean lamb of all sinews and marinate in one of the bowls for at least 15 minutes before cooking. On a grill plate, cook the lamb to medium-rare. Remove from grill, place in the second bowl of marinade and allow to rest for at least 5 minutes.

CAVALO NERO

Heat oil in a wok or frying pan and fry the merguez slices. Add the cavalo nero, stirring quickly. Remove from the heat, season and put aside on a tray.

To serve, put slow roasted onions on the plate and place the sliced lamb loin on top. Give the marinade that the lamb has been resting in a good stir and coat the meat. Sprinkle the cavalo nero, merguez and orange segments on top. This is a very quick dish to plate up as long as you have the onions ready.

NOTE: Saltbush lamb is grazed on the unique native pastures of the pristine Riverina district of New South Wales, Australia, which gives their meat a unique flavour.

SERVES 4

ve

Beef &
Venison

CALVESLIVERFOIE GRASSTYLE

This recipe is a replica of a dish we created with seared fresh duck foie gras. The same principle is used here using calves liver and the result is quite amazing. Make sure the liver is a blond and pale colour, not a deep dark one, and is very fresh with a firm texture. The caramelised turnips bring an element of sourness to break the richness of the liver and the lilly pilly capers, which are a native little red berry, give a natural acidity without using too much vinegar.

1 calf liver, skin and sinew removed, cut into ½cm (¼ in) slices

2 tablespoons caster sugar

2 tablespoons butter plus 50g (1²/₃ oz) extra

1 turnip, peeled and finely sliced

salt and pepper

1½ bunches baby spinach

3 tablespoons hazelnut oil

¹/₃ corn cob

4 shallots, sliced

3 garlic cloves, sliced

75g (2½ oz) bacon, cut into small batons

150g (5 oz) mushrooms, sliced finely

1 tablespoon lilly pilly or regular capers, rinsed (see Pantry)

1 tablespoon balsamic vinegar

1½ tablespoons coarsely chopped parsley

In a pan, caramelise sugar to a light blond colour. Add a knob of butter, turnip and season and keep stirring until turnip is cooked and lightly caramelised. Keep warm. Blanch the spinach in boiling water or stir-fry very quickly in a wok with a knob of butter.

In a large frying pan, heat the hazelnut oil, season and quickly sear the liver on both sides, keeping in mind they cook very fast and you want to keep them pink on the inside. Reserve. In the same pan add the corn, shallots, garlic, bacon and mushrooms with 50g (1²/₃ oz) butter. Cook on high heat very quickly, then add capers, balsamic vinegar, parsley and season with salt and pepper.

To serve, place spinach on plates, top with calves liver and spoon generously with the condiments and natural juices from the pan. Serve with a little bundle of turnips on the side.

NOTE: For a more intense taste, use wild mushrooms such as Slippery Jack or Pine mushrooms when they are in season.

SERVES 4–6

STEAKDIANE CUISINEDUTEMPS

This is a very special dish which we created in memory of the big steak with a fried egg on top and deglazed with vinegar, but incorporating an Asian influence for a more modestly portioned dish. The omelette filling is crunchy and fragrant. If your budget allows it, choose Wagyu quality beef.

400g (14 oz) eye fillet or sirloin in 4 pieces

MARINADE
250ml (8 fl oz) hoisin sauce (see Pantry)
2 tablespoons caster sugar
2 tablespoons soy sauce
75–100ml (2½–3½ fl oz) shaoxing wine (see Pantry)

DEGLAZING LIQUIDS
125ml (4 fl oz) chicken stock
70ml (2½ fl oz) mirin (see Pantry)
50ml (1¾ fl oz) light soy sauce
1½ tablespoons oyster sauce
¼ teaspoon sesame oil

OMELETTE MIX
3 eggs
2 tablespoons grapeseed oil
½ tablespoon mirin
1 tablespoon soy sauce
¼ teaspoon nuoc nam (see Pantry)

OMELETTE GARNISH
100g (3½ oz) bean shoots
8 cooked shiitakes (see Pantry), finely sliced
2 spring onions, finely sliced
1 tablespoon coriander/cilantro leaves, picked
1 birdseye chilli, deseeded and finely sliced
1 teaspoon ginger, julienned and blanched

MARINADE
Mix all ingredients together.

DEGLAZING LIQUIDS
Mix all ingredients together.

OMELETTE MIX
Break the eggs with a fork but don't work them too much. Add the other ingredients and mix gently.

Marinate the beef for 15 minutes before cooking. When ready to cook, add a touch of oil to a frying pan and cook to your liking. Once cooked, remove the meat and set aside. Add deglazing liquid to the pan and reduce quickly to a glossy and syrupy texture. Coat the meat generously.

OMELETTE GARNISH
Heat up a large non-stick frying pan with a touch of grapeseed oil. When hot, pour omelette mix in, keeping a thin layer so that it cooks very quickly and it's not too rich. Place garnish on top and roll omelette. Cut ends off and place on top of the meat. You can serve with a nice salad of small herbs such as coriander and watercress.

SERVES 4

TIANOFSHREDDED OXTAIL,POTATOAIOLI ANDCRISPYPARMESAN

OXTAIL

2 yearling oxtails cut osso bucco style into 3cm–4cm (1 in–1½ in) pieces

1 carrot, thickly sliced

1 stick celery, thickly sliced

1 onion, thickly sliced

½ leek, thickly sliced

3 garlic cloves, crushed

5 cardamom pods

3 star-anise

3 cloves

½ teaspoon juniper berries

1 teaspoon black peppercorns

2 tablespoons grated palm sugar

80ml (2¾ fl oz) malt vinegar

300ml (10½ fl oz) red wine

1 tablespoon nuoc nam (see Pantry)

400 ml (12½ fl oz) chicken stock

1 bouquet garni (see Pantry)

60ml (2 fl oz) soy sauce

Preheat oven to 150°C (300°F, Gas Mark 2). Heat a flame-proof baking dish with a lid on the stovetop with a little oil. Very gently seal the oxtail until golden brown all over and set aside.

Using the same pot, panfry the carrot, celery, onion, leek and garlic until the vegetables are slightly coloured. Add the spices, then the palm sugar and caramelise. Deglaze with malt vinegar and reduce the sauce a little. Add red wine, nuoc nam, stock, bouquet garni and soy sauce. Skim off excess oil.

Place the baking dish in the oven and cook with lid on for 3–4 hours or until meat falls off the bone. Let cool in stock. Pick meat from the bone making sure to remove all signs of sinew and hard cartilage. Place the meat in a bowl and keep moist with a little of the cooking liquid.

Reduce the rest of the cooking liquid to sauce consistency and strain through a fine strainer.

POTATO AIOLI

4 medium desiree potatoes

3 cloves garlic, cooked in 50ml (1¾ fl
  oz) olive oil

60g (2 oz) butter, soft

50ml (1¾ fl oz) cream

salt and pepper, to season

POTATO AIOLI

Steam the potatoes until tender. Pass through a potato mouli or mash.

Bring cream to a simmer in a small saucepan, don't boil, and add garlic, butter and finish with some of the olive oil used for cooking the garlic but keep the aioli quite firm. Season with salt and pepper.

To serve, fill cylinder tube moulds, about 5cm (2 in) in diameter, halfway to the top with potato aioli. Heat oxtail in a small saucepan, you may need to add more cooking juices, and top the mould up with oxtail mix. At the restaurant we put a disc-shaped Crispy Parmesan Tuille (see Basic Recipes) on the mould, place the sautéed mushrooms on top and finish with spring onion curls. Serve with sauce around the tian.

SERVES 4

Tian of shredded oxtail, potato aioli and crispy parmesan

Milk-fed veal in dashi with blue fin tuna natural

MILKFEDVEALINDASHI, BLUEFINTUNANATURAL

1 milk-fed veal fillet 650–700g
(1lb 5 oz–1lb 6½ oz), cut into
8 medallions

200g (6½ oz) sashimi grade blue fin
tuna, sliced into 12

3 tablespoons extra virgin olive oil

1 teaspoon lime juice

KOMBU AND DASHI STOCK

300ml (9 fl oz) dashi stock (see Basic
Recipes)

2 pieces kombu 4cm x 2cm (1½ in x ¾
in)

2 pieces orange peel, no white pith

2 pieces lemon peel

VEAL DRESSING

15ml (½ fl oz) lemon juice

75ml (2½ fl oz) extra virgin olive oil

drop sesame oil

1 teaspoon capers, rinsed

½ teaspoon liguria olives, pitted and cut

1 teaspoon chives, finely chopped
into very small dice

salt and pepper, to taste

KOMBU AND DASHI STOCK

In a saucepan big enough to fit the veal, add all the stock
ingredients and heat to 55°C–60°C (130°F–140°F).

Season veal and seal both sides in a lightly oiled frypan. Rest
in warm dashi stock until required.

VEAL DRESSING

In a bowl, mix all liquids well. Add capers, olives and chives
and season to taste. Set aside.

APPLE AND DAIKON SALAD

Combine all ingredients in a bowl. Check the balance of
flavours so one ingredient doesn't dominate, adjust if necessary
and season to taste. Set aside.

TOGAROSHI PANKO

In a wok, heat clarified butter to 160°C (320°F). Add the
panko and stir continuously until a nice golden colour is
achieved. Drain on absorbent paper and place in a bowl. Add
the togaroshi gradually and mix well.

APPLE AND DAIKON SALAD

1 tablespoon grated granny smith apple

1 tablespoon grated daikon (see Pantry)

1 teaspoon rice wine vinegar (see Pantry)

2 drops sesame oil

salt and pepper

TOGAROSHI PANKO

1 tablespoon clarified butter (see Pantry)

2 tablespoons panko (see Pantry)

¼ teaspoon togaroshi (see Pantry)

ZUCCHINI

1 green zucchini/courgette

dash of olive oil

salt and pepper

ZUCCHINI

Slice zucchini/courgette very thinly, lengthways, on a mandoline. Cut into 4cm (1½ in) lengths. Lie on a flat steamer tray, drizzle with a little olive oil and season. Steam for 2 minutes, then set aside and keep at room temperature. The zucchini is used as a base for the tuna so the tuna does not come in direct contact with the plate and retains its raw texture.

TO SERVE

Place the zucchini/courgette on one half of the plate and arrange the tuna on top. If you have a blowtorch, sear the tuna lightly, otherwise leave it raw. Dress the tuna with olive oil and lime juice. Place the veal next to the tuna, spoon over veal dressing and top with apple and daikon salad. Sprinkle with togaroshi panko, which adds an element of crispness.

SERVES 4

SANCHO VENISON WITH CAULIFLOWER, HORSERADISH GRIBICHE

I get really excited by the venison, sancho and wasabi flavour combination, it's very satisfying for a chef. What a lift it gives to the light but gamey flavour of the meat. Combined with cauliflower and horseradish, it is honestly a dish in perfect flavour harmony.

400g (13 oz) cleaned venison loin

salt

1 tablespoon grapeseed oil

SANCHO SEASONING MIX

1 teaspoon fennel seeds

½ teaspoon cardamom pods

1½ teaspoons coriander seeds

2 teaspoons black peppercorns

1 teaspoon sancho (see Pantry)

HORSERADISH EGG DRESSING

2 garlic cloves, poached in milk until soft, rinsed

1 egg, simmered for 4 minutes, peeled and refreshed in cold water

½ tablespoon fresh horseradish roots, finely grated

2 teaspoons Dijon mustard

½ teaspoon pickled ginger, finely chopped

3 teaspoons wasabi paste

1 tablespoon rice wine vinegar (see Pantry)

1 teaspoon fish sauce (see Pantry)

1 tablespoon mirin (see Pantry)

150ml (5¼ fl oz) vegetable oil

20ml (7 fl oz) sour cream

SANCHO SEASONING MIX

In a small frying pan, place all ingredients except the sancho and gently warm to release the flavour of each spice—about 4 minutes. Add the sancho. When all the spices are roasted, transfer to a mortar and pestle or spice grinder and grind into a coarse powder.

Season venison with salt and the sancho mix—there is no need to use extra pepper to season as the sancho seasoning already contains black pepper. In a lightly oiled frying pan, evenly sear the venison. Remove from pan and allow to rest for 5 minutes.

HORSERADISH EGG DRESSING

Combine garlic, egg, horseradish, mustard, ginger, wasabi and blitz in a food processor. Then add vinegar, fish sauce and mirin and drizzle in the oil until totally emulsified (combined). Add sour cream and season if needed.

STEAMED CAULIFLOWER

1 small head cauliflower, stems
  discarded
salt and pepper

GRIBICHE CONDIMENTS

1 egg, simmered for 12 minutes, peeled
  and refreshed in cold water
¼ red onion, brunoise
1 tablespoon chives, fine brunoise
1 tablespoon capers, washed thoroughly
  to remove excess salt

STEAMED CAULIFLOWER

Cut into florets, steam for 8–10 minutes and season. Set aside.

GRIBICHE CONDIMENTS

Separate cooked yolk and eggwhite and pass them separately through a coarse sieve. Mix all ingredients together and put aside until ready to serve.

TO SERVE

Warm the cauliflower in a steamer and place in the centre of the plate. Add a good spoonful of horseradish egg dressing on top. Top with gribiche condiments. Slice and arrange seared venison to the side.

SERVES 4

Sancho venison with cauliflower, horseradish gribiche

SANCH
WITHC
HORSE
GRIBIC

Pa

GNOCCHI

rock salt

2 sebago potatoes, 200g each (6½ oz), washed, skins on

60g (2 oz) plain/all purpose flour, plus extra for kneading the dough

1 egg yolk

pinch salt

5 tablespoons clarified butter (see Pantry)

1 tablespoon grated parmesan

salt and pepper to season

1 tablespoon butter, to serve

Heat oven to 180°C (350°F, Gas Mark 4). Cover baking tray with 1cm (½in) thick layer of rock salt and place whole potatoes on top. Cook in oven until soft, about 2 hours. Remove from oven and push them through a drum sieve, discarding skins. Place cooked potato flesh in a large bowl and sprinkle in flour, being careful not to add it all at once. Work the potato and flour mixture into a dough, adding more flour if necessary, being careful not to overwork. Add egg yolk and salt and work into mixture. Roll the dough into a cylinder approximately 1cm in diameter and cut into small pillow-shaped pieces. In a saucepan, bring water to a simmer and drop gnocchi into the water. When they float to the top, remove using a slotted spoon and refresh in a bowl of ice water.

TO SERVE

Melt clarified butter in a small frying pan and add gnocchi, frying gently until slightly golden on both sides. Place in a bowl, sprinkle with parmesan, salt and pepper and add a knob of fresh butter.

NOTE: The most important thing when making gnocchi is that the potatoes and the dough remain warm the entire time you are working with them to keep them moist and soft. Be generous with the clarified butter when you fry the gnocchi before serving.

SERVES 4

Pushing potatoes for gnocchi through a drum sieve

Adding egg yolks to gnocchi dough

LEMONPASTA

1 teaspoon dried lemon zest (see method)

250g (8 oz) plain/all purpose flour

1 tablespoon salt

1 tablespoon olive oil

2 eggs

1 egg yolk

To make the dried lemon zest, peel the lemons, remove white pith and slice very finely Dry in a oven on very low heat for a minimum of 2 hours, being careful not to let the skin colour or burn. When dried, blitz in a spice grinder.

In a food processor, blitz flour, salt and olive oil. Stop the processor, add eggs and yolk, then pulse until the mixture becomes crumbly. Remove from processor and start to knead. Roll out with a rolling pin.

Feed the pasta through a pasta machine, every time you put it through fold it and place it through again. This makes the pasta stronger and shiny. Pass it through the machine until it is ½–2mm thick. Cut into 30cm (12 in) lengths about the size of an A4 sheet.

Bring a large pot of salted water to the boil. Blanch the pasta sheets gently until al dente, this will only take a minute or two. Refresh under cold water.

See page 148 for pictures.

The pasta can then be cut into shapes to be used for spaghetti, fettucine, tagliatelle or pappardelle.

SERVES 4

SPAETZLE

100g (3½ oz) plain/all purpose flour
2 eggs
salt
50ml (1¾ fl oz) milk

In a bowl, combine flour, eggs and salt. Add milk, beating to achieve a smooth batter-like consistency. Put mixture into a plastic piping bag with a small nozzle. Bring large pot of salted water to a simmer, and pipe batter in a continuous line into the pot, cook for approximately 1 minute. Refresh in iced water and allow to drain on a lightly oiled paper towel. This will prevent spaetzle sticking to the paper. You can use spaetzle as you would any pasta. For variety, you can deep-fry the spaetzle, which puff up and become very crispy. This is how I prefer to use them. Once cooked and refreshed, if you find it too long, it can be cut into smaller pieces.

SERVES 4

SQUID**INK**PASTA

2 eggs

1 egg yolk

2 tablespoons squid ink (available from fishmonger), passed through a fine sieve

250g (8 oz) plain/all purpose flour

½ tablespoon olive oil

In a bowl, lightly whisk eggs, egg yolk, and squid ink to combine. Place the flour in a food processor, add the egg and squid ink and mix. Then add the oil and continue mixing until it becomes like breadcrumbs (about 5–10 seconds). Remove from the processor and work mixture altogether into a dough.

Using a rolling pin, roll the dough until it can fit through a pasta machine, then laminate.

This pasta can be cut into desired shape depending what you will use this pasta for—lasagna, ravioli, tagliatelle or spaghettini. This is very easy to do, and will get much interest from your guests or family.

NOTE: I never rest my pasta dough, I like to use it straightaway. I can laminate to a much thinner layer. I don't have to put too much flour when I work it and I find I retain a much firmer texture and a perfect smoothness.

NOTE: Squid ink is very salty so don't season with salt.

SERVES 4

AUSTRALIAN BLACK TRUFFLE AGNOLOTTI WITH MUSHROOM BROTH

Australia is now producing some of the best black truffles—tuber melanosporum—in Western Australia and Tasmania. Production is still in the early stages, but the results so far are exceptional, and I have no hesitation in putting them on a par with the French variety.

FILLING

rock salt

400g (13 oz) desiree potatoes, brushed, skin on

1 tablespoon hazelnut oil

2 tablespoons extra virgin olive oil

60g (2 oz) butter

1 white salad onion, finely sliced

1 tablespoon olive oil

2 garlic cloves, diced small

2 tablespoons kaiser fleisch (see Pantry), diced small

50ml (1¾ fl oz) cream

Australian black truffle (as much as your budget can afford), diced small

½ tablespoon parsley, chopped

salt and pepper, to season

TO MAKE THE FILLING

Line a baking tray with 1cm (½ in) layer of rock salt, place the potatoes on the salt and bake in the oven at 200°C (400°F, Gas Mark 6) until soft, approximately 2 hours. Once cooked, pass through a drum sieve, discarding skin. While the potato is still hot, fold through the hazelnut and olive oils and butter. This is best done with a wooden spoon, as using a mouli or food processor can make the potatoes waxy. In a large saucepan, sweat the onion with 1 tablespoon of olive oil until translucent, add garlic and kaiserfleisch and toss quickly together. Add the cream and remove from heat immediately. Once mixture has cooled to room temperature, add the truffle and parsley. Fold through the potato mix and season with salt and pepper.

PASTA DOUGH

500g (1 lb) plain/all purpose flour
6 egg yolks
3 eggs
2 tablespoons olive oil
salt
shaved parmesan, to garnish

MUSHROOM BROTH

See Soups

FOR PASTA

Process the flour with the yolks, eggs and olive oil for no longer than 20 seconds or it will form a ball. Season and remove from mixer, then roll the pasta dough out into long and thin sheets. To fill the pasta, place mixture along one side (½ tablespoon for large agnolotti or 1 teaspoon for small agnolotti), moisten with water, fold over and close to form the agnolotti shape. To cook, bring a saucepan of water to boil, reduce to simmer, add agnolotti and blanch for 20 seconds, do not boil as this will ruin your pasta, it will go puffy and soft and may become stodgy. Remove from saucepan and place into a bowl of ice water to refresh. The agnolotti can also be frozen for later use.

TO SERVE

Reheat, steam or blanch the agnolotti until hot. Place in bowl and add mushroom broth, aerating before serving with a stick blender until light and frothy. Garnish with shaved parmesan and any leftover truffle slices.

SERVES 8–10

Australian black truffle agnolotti with mushroom broth

BEETROOT**RAVIOLI**

With the red beetroot juice of the ravioli running through the black pasta, this is a very dramatic and tasty dish.

1½ tablespoons palm sugar

1 teaspoon onion seeds

35–40ml (1½ fl oz) rice wine vinegar (see Pantry)

½ beetroot, brunoise

½ beetroot, processed to a juice with 125ml (4 fl oz) water

salt and pepper

1½ gelatine leaves

Squid ink pasta (see Squid Ink Pasta in this section)

In a saucepan, gently caramelise the palm sugar, add the onion seeds and stir until fragrant.

Add the rice wine vinegar and reduce to make a balanced gastric. Stir until sugar is completely dissolved. Add the beetroot, beetroot juice, salt and pepper and reduce by half until the beetroot is cooked al dente. Remove the mixture from the heat and add the gelatine. Allow to set in the fridge for 1–2 hours. Once set, spoon a teaspoon of mixture into some squid ink pasta and roll into a ravioli. To cook, see directions in Australian Black Truffle Agnolotti in this section.

SERVES 4

Veget

ables

MUSHROOMS WITH EARTHY FLAVOURS AND HAZELNUTS

Mushrooms are one of my favourite vegetables, and I can honestly say this mushroom dish is the best I have ever tasted. These are ideal for breakfast.

50g (1²/₃ oz) butter

8 Swiss brown field mushrooms or, in autumn, wild mushrooms

3 garlic cloves, sliced

3 golden shallots, sliced

2 tablespoons roasted hazelnuts, chopped

6 sprigs wild thyme

80g (2²/₃ oz) parmesan shavings

3 tablespoons extra virgin olive oil

2 tablespoons hazelnut oil

salt and pepper, to taste

Preheat oven to 180°C (350°F, Gas Mark 4). On a sheet of aluminum foil, dab little knobs of butter and place the mushrooms on top.

On each mushroom, place a slice each of garlic, shallots, hazelnuts, thyme and parmesan. Drizzle with the oils and season with salt and pepper to taste.

Cover with another sheet of aluminum foil and seal the 2 sheets together. Bake in oven for 12 minutes.

SERVES 2–4

BORLOTTIAND TRUFFLEPUREE

½ cup borlotti beans (if using dried beans, soak overnight in water with a pinch of salt)

1 large potato (equal to double the amount of the borlotti beans)

60ml (2 fl oz) cream

50g (1²/₃ oz) butter

1 teaspoon of truffle oil (see Pantry)

black truffles, as many as you like

salt and pepper, to taste

In a large saucepan of seasoned water, cook the borlotti beans until tender. Meanwhile, cut potato into chunks, and cook separately in seasoned water. When both the beans and potato are very soft, strain and pass through a fine drum sieve and set aside.

In a small saucepan, bring cream and butter to a gentle simmer.

Combine the potatoes and beans in a large bowl. Fold through the cream and butter until the mixture is smooth, but not too runny. Drizzle in a little truffle oil and fold through the truffle pieces, being careful not to overpower the puree with the truffle oil. Season with salt and pepper to taste.

SERVES 4

EMBEURRÉE OFCABBAGE

2 tablespoons olive oil

few coriander/cilantro seeds

few black peppercorns

¼ onion, medium diced

2 garlic cloves, crushed

2 tablespoons kaiserfleisch (see Pantry), or smoky bacon, cut into batons or thin slices

3 tablespoons butter

¼ savoy cabbage, tear the leaves into quarters and discard the stem and any thick veins

In a saucepan, heat the oil and fry coriander/cilantro seeds and pepper until fragrant, take out and discard. Use the same saucepan to sweat off the onion and garlic until soft, add the kaiserfleisch and gently fry for 1 minute to extract the smoky flavour. Add half the butter, then the cabbage and the rest of the butter last. Cook at high heat for 2 minutes without stirring. Stir well for another minute, then remove cabbage leaves from saucepan and lay on a tray to cool. The cabbage leaves should still be slightly firm and translucent. Season. Serve with meat or poultry.

NOTE: For vegetarians, replace the kaiserfleisch with daikon pieces.

SERVES 4–6

BORLOTTIBEANS

½ cup fresh borlotti beans

150ml (4½ fl oz) olive oil

½ teaspoon coriander/cilantro seeds

½ teaspoon peppercorns

1 bay leaf

2 sprigs thyme

1 clove garlic

GARNISH

3 baby carrots

4 asparagus

2 tablespoons semi-dried tomatoes

In a saucepan, place the borlotti beans and cover with water. Simmer until tender, strain but don't refresh, and put aside.

In a separate saucepan, heat the olive oil and place in the remaining ingredients. Heat to approx 55°C (110°F) and cook until fragrant. Cool slightly and add the beans. Heat just before serving and add a little of each garnish.

GARNISH

Cut the carrot and asparagus finely on an angle, blanch and refresh.

SERVES 4

BRAISEDSILVERBEET

2 tablespoons caster sugar

½ bunch silverbeet stalks, peeled and
   sliced on an angle down the stalk

½ onion, sliced

2 garlic cloves, crushed

1 tablespoon vegetable oil

zest of 1 lemon

5 juniper berries

6 black peppercorns

200ml (7 fl oz) white wine

80ml (2¾ fl oz) vinegar

50g (1²/₃ oz) butter, cubed

light soy sauce to taste

Preheat oven to 175°C (350°F, Gas Mark 4). In a shallow pan, lightly caramelise the sugar. Add the silverbeet and stir well. Transfer the silverbeet to a baking tray and season.

In a separate saucepan, sweat off the onion and garlic in the oil and place on top of the silverbeet. Place the zest, juniper berries and peppercorns on top of the onion and garlic.

In another pan, bring liquids to the boil and pour over the silverbeet. Place butter on top, cover with baking paper and put in oven until just cooked al dente.

Serve with red game meat such as venison, hare or pigeon, or a boiled corned beef girello (silverside).

SERVES 4

PEPPERED WATERMELON WITH PUMPKIN AND COCONUT CURRY

The seared and peppered watermelon adds much interest to this light pumpkin curry. This is a dish with a lot of flavour and is very quick to put together.

CURRY

1 tablespoon oil

½ teaspoon black mustard seeds

¼ cumin seeds

4 curry leaves

150g (5oz) pumpkin, diced into cubes

pinch of asafoetida (see Pantry)

2 teaspoons grated palm sugar

½ teaspoon fresh grated turmeric or
  ground turmeric

1 small knob ginger, finely sliced

salt and pepper, to taste

1 small red chilli, deseeded

juice and zest of ½ lime

150ml (5¼ fl oz) fresh coconut cream

50g (1¾ oz) fresh tomatoes, diced

2 tablespoons coriander/cilantro leaves

1 tablespoon sliced spring onions

WATERMELON

8 batons of watermelon, 6cm x 1cm
  (2½ in x ¼ in)

2 teaspoons cracked white pepper

2 teaspoons vegetable oil

2 handfuls snow pea/mange tout tendrils

1 teaspoon olive oil

Heat oil in a wok, fry mustard seed, cumin and curry leaves until fragrant. Add pumpkin, asafoetida, palm sugar, turmeric, ginger, salt and pepper and cook at medium heat for 3 minutes. Add chilli, zest and juice of lime and coconut milk. Bring to simmering point and cook until the pumpkin is al dente, this won't take very long. Take the wok off the heat, add diced tomato and sprinkle with coriander/cilantro leaves and spring onion. Place in a serving bowl.

Coat the watermelon with the cracked pepper and fry quickly in a frying pan with vegetable oil until fragrant and translucent.

Spoon the pumpkin curry into serving bowls with watermelon. Dress snow pea tendril with olive oil and place on top of the dish.

SERVES 4

VEGETABLE BHAJI AND CORIANDER CHUTNEY

The crispiness of the vegetables makes this dish exciting.

2L (64 fl oz) peanut oil, for frying

30g (1 oz) of various fresh vegetables (such as carrot, zucchini/courgette, celery, okra, cucumber and capsicum/sweet pepper), cut into long strips

1 nori sheet cut into 5mm (¼ in)-wide strips

100g (3½ oz) rice flour

BATTER

100g (3½ oz) chickpea flour

pinch of chilli powder

½ teaspoon turmeric powder

2 curry leaves, finely diced

pinch of bicarbonate of soda

¼ teaspoon black mustard seed

¼ teaspoon fenugreek seed

¼ teaspoon cumin seed

50ml (1¾ fl oz) soda water

pinch of salt

CORIANDER CHUTNEY

¼ onion, finely sliced

2 garlic cloves, crushed

½ teaspoon grated ginger

½ teaspoon sugar

½ teaspoon lemon or lime juice

20 mint leaves

½ bunch coriander/cilantro leaves

vegetable oil, to blend

BATTER

In a mixing bowl, mix flour, chilli powder, turmeric, curry leaves and bicarbonate of soda and set aside.

In a small frying pan, dry roast the mustard, fenugreek and cumin seeds. Let cool, then add to the flour mixture. Add the soda water and salt. Use a fork or chopstick rather than a whisk to mix, ignoring lumps in batter.

In a wok, heat the peanut oil. Make 4–8 bundles of vegetables and tie them together with a strip of nori. Roll in the rice flour and dip each vegetable bundle into the batter. Deep fry until golden. Remove and drain on a paper towel.

Serve hot with coriander chutney.

CORIANDER CHUTNEY

Place all ingredients except the oil in a food processor and blitz, adding the oil in a slow steady stream until you have a smooth paste.

SERVES 4

Vegetable bhaji and coriander chutney

VEGE

ANDO

CHUT

SOFTPOLENTA WITHPARMESAN ANDSAFFRON

1L (32 fl oz) water

150g (5 oz) medium grain polenta

200ml (7 oz) milk

80g (2^2/$_3$ oz) finely grated parmesan

50g (1^2/$_3$ oz) butter

pinch of saffron powder

salt and pepper, to taste

In a medium pot, bring the water to the boil. Add the polenta, whisking continually, then add the milk gradually to achieve a thick and smooth consistency. When the polenta has lost its graininess, it is ready to add parmesan, saffron and butter. Season to taste. Serve with osso bucco, venison or beef.

SERVES 4–6

MILDSPICEDLENTILS

2 teaspoons olive oil
1 garlic clove, crushed
½ celery stick, sliced
1 small red chilli, deseeded
½ cinnamon stick
150g (5 oz) French green lentils
zest of ½ orange
250ml (8 fl oz) chicken stock
salt and pepper, to taste

In a saucepan, heat oil and sweat garlic, celery, chilli and cinnamon until the fragrance of the spices is released.

Add lentils, orange zest and chicken stock. Season and cook at a gentle simmer until the lentils are soft, approximately 15 minutes.

These tasty lentils can be served hot or cold as a salad.

NOTE: For vegetarians, substitute water or vegetable stock for chicken stock.

SERVES 4–6

PICKLED WOMBOK

A fresher, more textured alternative to traditional sauerkraut.

½ wombok (see Pantry)

1 salad onion, sliced

½ teaspoon of black peppercorns, lightly crushed

1 tablespoon clarified butter

125ml (4 fl oz) white vinegar

125ml (4 fl oz) white wine

1 bay leaf

2 stalks thyme

3 juniper berries

2 garlic cloves, crushed

75ml (2½ fl oz) chicken stock

pinch of salt

Separate the leaves and stalks of the wombok. Slice the stalks thinly on an angle.

In a medium sized saucepan, sweat onion and pepper in a little clarified butter until soft. Add vinegar and reduce until almost evaporated. Add white wine, bay leaf, thyme, juniper berries and garlic and reduce by half. Add chicken stock to taste. Season with a pinch of salt.

To cook wombok, bring pickling liquid to the boil and pour over the wombok. Remove from liquid to serve. Can be served with milk-fed veal, steamed fish or tea-smoked chicken.

SERVES 4–6

TARRAGON
RATATOUILLE

A powerfully flavoured variation on cooking and presenting traditional ratatouille.

½L (16 fl oz) peanut oil

4 red capsicums/sweet peppers, deseeded and cut in half

4 orange capsicums/sweet peppers, deseeded and diced

2 tomatoes, quartered and seeded

1 bunch small white salad onions

4 gourmet eggplants/aubergine, sliced (also known as finger or Lebanese eggplant)

3 small zucchinis/courgettes, sliced

2 green jalapeño chillies, deseeded and julienned

4 garlic cloves, whole

3 sprigs fresh tarragon

salt and pepper, to taste

1 small orange, juiced

100ml (3½ fl oz) extra virgin olive oil

1 teaspoon caster sugar

½ teaspoon salt flakes

4 sprigs of wild thyme

1 tablespoon roasted pine nuts

1 tablespoon finely sliced chives

In a small wok, heat the peanut oil and fry the whole capsicum/sweet pepper until the skin blisters. Place in a mixing bowl and cover tightly with a sheet of cling film, let them rest for 15 minutes. Once rested, the skins should peel off very easily. Halve and remove seeds. Cut the tomatoes into quarters, deseed. Peel and trim the salad onions until they are the size of a quail egg.

In a small baking tray or baking dish lay the sweet peppers, eggplant, zucchini/courgette, jalapeños, garlic and salad onions, place the fresh tarragon on top and season lightly. Pour over the orange juice and cover with a sheet of baking paper. Place the tomato quarters on top of the baking paper, coat lightly with olive oil and sprinkle with the sugar, flaked salt and wild thyme.

Place in an oven on a low heat 120°C (250°F, Gas Mark 1) and cook for 1 hour. The tomatoes will shrink and their flavour will become concentrated, with a hint of wild thyme.

TO SERVE

Arrange all the vegetables around each other (discard the tarragon). Whisk all the cooking juices to blend well and spoon over the vegetables. Sprinkle with the pine nuts and the chives.

SERVES 4

KOHLRABI BARIGOULE

120ml (4 fl oz) olive oil

2 sprigs thyme

1 fresh bay leaf

6 black peppercorns

6 coriander/cilantro seeds

½ cinnamon stick

2 cardamom pods

1 kohlrabi (see Pantry)

1 shallot, sliced

2 cloves garlic, sliced

1 tablespoon duck fat

In a saucepan, gently fry thyme, bay leaf and spices in oil until fragrant. Meanwhile, peel kohlrabi back to the white flesh and halve from top to bottom, then halve again. Slice each quarter into thin slices on a mandolin. Let oil cool slightly, then add the shallots and garlic and sweat until cooked through.

Add duck fat and the kohlrabi and cook until al dente. Serve with beef fillet, chicken or duck.

NOTE: Kohlrabi is a member of the cabbage family and once cooked has a great texture and flavour.

SERVES 4

SANCHO COATED ZUCCHINI TEMPURA, CAULIFLOWER WITH HORSERADISH DRESSING

A very interesting vegetarian dish with balance of texture and flavours.

SANCHO ZUCCHINI

3 tablespoons olive oil
8 thin zucchini/courgette slices
pinch salt
pinch sancho (see Pantry)

ZUCCHINI FLOWER TEMPURA

2 zucchini/corgette flowers, inside stem
  removed
tempura batter (see Basic Recipes)
salt to taste

STEAMED CAULIFLOWER

½ small cauliflower, cut into large florets
salt and pepper, to taste

SANCHO ZUCCHINI

In a saucepan, heat the oil over a medium heat, season the zucchini/courgette with salt and sancho pepper and lightly sauté until al dente. Leave the zucchini/courgette in the olive oil and set aside.

ZUCCHINI FLOWER TEMPURA

Lightly and evenly coat the flowers in batter and deep fry. When cooked, the batter should be light and crispy, not thick and heavy. Season with salt and pepper to taste.

STEAMED CAULIFLOWER

Place cauliflower in a steamer for approximately 12 minutes or until tender, remove and season lightly with salt and pepper to taste.

HORSERADISH EGG DRESSING

2 garlic cloves, poached in milk until soft, and rinsed

1 egg, simmered for 4 minutes, peeled and refreshed in cold water

½ tablespoon fresh horseradish roots

2 teaspoons Dijon mustard

½ teaspoon pickled ginger, finely chopped

⅓ teaspoon wasabi paste (see Pantry)

1 tablespoon rice wine vinegar (see Pantry)

1 teaspoon fish sauce (see Pantry)

1 tablespoon mirin (see Pantry)

150ml (5¼ fl oz) vegetable oil

20ml (¾ fl oz) sour cream

GRIBICHE CONDIMENTS

1 egg, simmered for 12 minutes, peeled, refreshed in iced water and diced very finely

¼ red onion, cut into small dice and soaked in cold water for 5 minutes

½ bunch chives, sliced finely

1 tablespoon capers, washed thoroughly to remove excess salt

HORSERADISH EGG DRESSING

Combine garlic, egg, horseradish, mustard, ginger, wasabi and blitz in blender or food processor. Add vinegar, fish sauce and mirin and drizzle in the oil until thoroughly mixed. Add sour cream and season to taste.

GRIBICHE CONDIMENTS

In a bowl, mix all ingredients together and set aside.

To serve, place the cauliflower on a plate, spoon a large tablespoon of horseradish egg dressing on top and sprinkle with a teaspoon of the gribiche condiments.

SERVES 4

Sancho coated zucchini tempura, cauliflower with horseradish dressing

ANCHO

ZUCCHIN

CAULIFLO

HORSERA

DRESSIN

LACQUERED TOFU WITH MISO AND MARINATED CUCUMBERS

400g (13 oz) silky tofu cut into
  1.5cm (½ in) cubes
1 small Lebanese cucumber, sliced
  1.5cm x 5.5cm (²/₃ in x 2½ in)

MISO PASTE

75g (2½ oz) red miso (see Pantry)
1½ tablespoons white miso (see Pantry)
3 egg yolks
20ml (¹/₃ fl oz) sake
20ml (¹/₃ fl oz) mirin (see Pantry)
70ml (2½ fl oz) dashi stock (see Basic
  Recipes)
zest of ½ lime

LIME AND WASABI SOUR CREAM

zest and juice of ½ lime
¹/₃ cup sour cream
1 teaspoon wasabi paste (see Pantry)

MISO PASTE

In a saucepan, combine all ingredients except zest and cook on low heat until thickened to a sauce-like consistency, cool then add lime zest.

LIME AND WASABI SOUR CREAM

In a bowl, mix ingredients together, being careful not to whisk too vigorously so that you retain the texture of the sour cream.

CUCUMBER MARINADE

Peel of one orange, julienned

1 tablespoon Szechuan pepper (see Pantry)

1 tablespoon coriander/cilantro seeds

2 tablespoons palm sugar

3–4 teaspoons dried chilli

300ml (10½ fl oz) vegetable oil

1½ tablespoons ginger, julienned

350ml (11½ fl oz) white vinegar

COLESLAW

½ carrot peeled

2 fine red cabbage leaves

4 wombok leaves (see Pantry)

3 green spring onion stems

1 tablespoon coriander/cilantro leaves, or ½ tablespoon of micro coriander shoots (see Pantry)

1 tablespoon extra virgin olive oil

CUCUMBER MARINADE

Place all ingredients except vinegar in a saucepan and bring to the boil. As mixture cools, add the vinegar. Two minutes before serving, place cucumber in the marinade.

COLESLAW

Cut each of the vegetables into a very fine julienne. Soak cut carrot and spring onion in ice water so they remain crisp. Drain well, and mix all vegetables together.

TO SERVE

Coat the top of the tofu with a thin layer of miso paste and place under grill for 1 minute or until the miso paste starts to caramelise, this will take approximately 2 minutes. Once it is nicely lacquered, remove from grill and place three pieces of tofu per person on a plate. Top each piece of tofu with a slice of marinated cucumber. Spoon sour cream onto the cucumber. Dress coleslaw with a little olive oil, and place a small bundle on top of the cucumber. To add a crunchy texture, top with a Brik Pastry Tuille (see Basic Recipes).

SERVES 4–6

Lacquered tofu with miso and marinated cucumbers

LACQU
WITHM
MARIN
CUCUM

eese

BLUECHEESEAND PARMESANTART, PICKLEDLAMB TONGUESALAD

BLUE CHEESE TART

100g (3½ oz) roquefort cheese

100g (3½ oz) soft fresh sheep's milk cheese

130ml (4 fl oz) vegetable stock (see Basic Recipes)

2 gelatine leaves, softened in cold water

160g (5¼ oz) cream, whipped to soft peaks

TURMERIC AND ZUCCHINI DRESSING

3 tablespoons grapeseed oil

3 teaspoons mirin (see Pantry)

2 teaspoons light soy sauce

¼ teaspoon grated turmeric

2 tablespoons green zucchini/courgette skins, finely diced

2 teaspoons carrot, finely diced

½ large shallot, finely diced

½ garlic clove, finely diced

2 teaspoons rice wine vinegar (see Pantry)

2 teaspoons finely sliced chives

GARNISH

4 Cripsy Parmesan Tuile (see Basic Recipes)

4 cooked pickled suckling lamb tongues, finely sliced (available from gourmet markets or good delicatessens)

1 teaspoon shiso micro herbs (available from Asian grocery stores) (see Pantry)

1 tablespoon young rocket salad

BLUE CHEESE TART

Keep both cheeses in a warm place until ready to use. Pass through a sieve using a plastic spatula into a medium-sized bowl.

Heat vegetable broth to a gentle simmer. Add the gelatine leaves and dissolve them in broth. Cool broth slightly and add to cheese, mixing over a bowl half filled with ice and water until well combined. When the cheese mixture thickens a little, fold through the cream. Leave on ice until it is the thickness of medium-whipped cream and pipe into moulds slightly greased with oil. Refrigerate to set.

TURMERIC AND ZUCCHINI DRESSING

Mix all ingredients together in a bowl.

GARNISH

Cook parmesan as for Crispy Parmesan and curl on a small rolling pin.

To serve, gently remove the cheese from the mould and place on the plate. Arrange the pickled lamb tongue on the side or on top of the cheese with the rocket and herbs. Drizzle with turmeric and zucchini dressing. Place the parmesan tuile on top.

NOTE: We use suckling lamb tongue for its delicate, natural sweetness, which goes very well with sheep's milk cheese.

SERVES 4

DELICE SOUFFLÉ OF FROMAGE BLANC

I created this recipe when my wife Kathy and I were running the family restaurant L' Hotel du Nord in Cuiseaux, the village where I was born in the beautiful region of Jura and Burgundy in France. Across the street from the restaurant was the cheese factory, La Fromagerie, where they made fresh fromage blanc everyday as well as the big wheels of gruyere. I wanted to create a recipe incorporating these two cheeses that I ate everyday as a child and that gave me so much pleasure.

SOUFFLÉ

400g (13 oz) of fromage blanc, quark or cottage cheese

6 level teaspoons of cornflour/cornstarch

salt and pepper, to taste

6 egg yolks

160g (5½ oz) gruyere or cheddar cheese, grated

6 eggwhites

DELICE

Gently fold together the fromage blanc, cornflour/cornstarch, salt and pepper. Once incorporated, add the egg yolks and the gruyere and combine very gently.

In a mixer, whisk the eggwhites to medium soft peaks. Fold the eggwhites into the cheese mixture, a third at a time, working it very gently each time.

Preheat oven to 180°C (350°F, Gas Mark 4). Generously butter soufflé moulds and fill them to 1cm (½ in) from the top. Place in a baking dish and fill the dish with water until it reaches halfway up the sides of the moulds. Place in oven and cook for approximately 25 minutes (18–20 minutes in a fan-forced oven). They should be golden brown. Remove soufflés from the baking dish, unmould onto a plate and serve with watercress sauce.

WATERCRESS SAUCE

1 bunch of watercress or choy sum,
  leaves only

100ml (3½ fl oz) vegetable stock (see
  Basic Recipes)

150ml (4½ fl oz) cream

pinch of paprika

salt and pepper, to taste

WATERCRESS SAUCE

Blanch the watercress leaves for 10 seconds in boiling water, do not refresh.

In a pot, bring vegetable stock to the boil, take off the heat and add the blanched watercress, then let infuse for 5 minutes. Add the cream and simmer gently, until the sauce has reduced by a quarter. Season with paprika, salt and pepper. Process the sauce with a stick blender to make it light and frothy. This sauce is very simple so as not to overwhelm the delicate flavour of the soufflé.

NOTE: If you don't use all the soufflés, unmould them all and refrigerate. Reheat them for about 10 minutes in a baking dish with about 150ml (4¼ fl oz) of milk. They will come back to their original size again and be as light and flavoursome as if just baked.

SERVES 4

Delice soufflé of fromage blanc

FRESH COTTAGE CHEESE AND ROQUEFORT MILLEFEUILLE WITH SPICED WALNUTS

FROMAGE MIX
60g (2 oz) roquefort cheese
250g (8 oz) fresh cottage cheese

SPICED WALNUTS
½ teaspoon walnut oil
1 handful of fresh walnut kernels
¼ teaspoon celery salt
pinch of Murray River or sea salt flakes
¼ teaspoon ground cinnamon
¼ teaspoon lightly smoked paprika
½ teaspoon caster sugar

12 seedless grapes, cut in half
1 tablespoon hazelnut oil
2 sheets brik pastry (see Basic Recipes)
4 truffled bush peaches (available from specialty stores, see Pantry)

Using two forks, break up the roquefort, then gently fold in the cottage cheese and set aside.

In a wok, gently heat up the walnut oil, add walnut kernels and stir until nicely toasted. Take the wok off the heat and drain excess oil but don't pat wok dry—a little moisture helps the spices to stick. Add spices and coat well. Remove from wok and place spice-coated walnuts on absorbent paper to eliminate residual oils.

In a small frying pan, slightly warm up the grapes with the hazelnut oil.

TO SERVE
Place the cheese mix between the sheets of pastry and serve with the warm grapes, spiced walnuts and bush peaches.

SERVES 4

FARMHOUSE CHEDDAR, BRAISED POTATOES AND TURMERIC CARROTS

In my childhood, we always used to eat steamed potatoes with warm or melted cheese, or with traditional cheese dishes of the Jura region as a raclette or fondue. I really enjoy eating potatoes with cheese, it gives them so much more elegance and lightness.

200g farmhouse cheddar or generic cheddar cheese

BRAISED POTATOES

500g (1lb) potatoes, cut into 4cm x 2cm (¾ in x 1½ in) thick pieces

150ml (5¼ fl oz) chicken stock

3 tablespoons light soy sauce

60g (2oz) butter

SPICED TURMERIC CARROTS

2 tablespoons palm sugar

¼ teaspoon Szechuan pepper (see Pantry)

½ cinnamon stick

3 green cardamom pods

2 tablespoons white vinegar

2 tablespoons light soy sauce

¼ teaspoon garlic, diced

½ teaspoon turmeric, freshly grated

50ml (1¾ fl oz) orange juice

1 carrot, julienned or shredded

BLACK GRAPE VINAIGRETTE

200g (6½ oz) black grapes

½ tablespoon rice vinegar

1 tablespoon verjuice (see Pantry)

BRAISED POTATOES

Preheat oven to 160°C (325°F, Gas Mark 2–3). Place the potatoes on a lined baking tray and pour over the stock and soy sauce. Cover with butter and bake in oven for about 30 minutes or until cooked. The potatoes should have absorbed most of the cooking liquids and be nicely glazed.

SPICED TURMERIC CARROTS

In a pan, caramelise the palm sugar over a moderate heat until it has liquefied, about 2 minutes. Add the Szechuan pepper, cinnamon and cardamom, and deglaze with the vinegar. Add the soy sauce, garlic, tumeric, orange juice and carrots and cook on high heat until al dente.

BLACK GRAPE VINAIGRETTE

Process grapes in a blender. Place in a saucepan and simmer until the juices are reduced by half. Strain through a fine sieve and add rice vinegar and verjuice.

TO SERVE

Cut the cheese into 1cm–2cm (½ in–1 in) long triangles, 1cm–2cm thick. Allowing 2 slices per serve, place cheese on top of potato. Place under a medium grill until it melts slightly. Serve with the turmeric carrots and grape vinaigrette.

SERVES 4

CLAFOUTIS OF CHERRIES AND PEARS

What is wonderful about this recipe is that, unlike a traditional clafoutis, there is no pastry. The sabayon is so light and spongy it's like eating a bowl of warm fruit.

FRUIT GARNISH

50g (1²/₃ oz) sugar

½ vanilla bean

½ cinnamon stick

2 star-anise

3 cloves

4 black peppercorns

300g (10 oz) fresh cherries, pitted

4 poached pears, cut in wedges

200ml (7 fl oz) berry coulis

knob of butter

sprinkle of sugar

CLAFOUTIS MIX

200ml (7 fl oz) milk

300ml (10½ fl oz) cream

8 eggs

240g (8 oz) sugar

60g (2 oz) flour

25ml (⁷/₈ fl oz) kirsch (see Pantry)

FRUIT GARNISH

In a saucepan, caramelise sugar with all the spices and deglaze with the berry coulis. Add the cherries and pears and cook, at very low heat for 5 minutes, reserve. Strain fruit. Grease the clafoutis moulds with butter, sprinkle with sugar and divide mixture amongst bowls.

CLAFOUTIS MIX

Preheat oven to 150°C–160°C (300°F–325°F, Gas Mark 2). In a saucepan, warm the milk and cream. Remove from heat and allow to cool. When milk and cream are cool, whisk the eggs, sugar and ¹/₃ (20g) of the flour together to make a sabayon. It should double in size. Add the rest of the flour. Fold the cream and milk into the sabayon and add the kirsch. Pour mixture over the fruit into the moulds and bake for about 25 minutes until mixture is set and golden.

TO SERVE

Leave in the moulds, dust with icing sugar and a scoop of vanilla ice-cream or coconut sorbet (see Ice-Creams & Sorbets).

NOTE: The cherries will taste better if you spice them the day before. You will need individual ovenproof bowls or ramekins for this dessert. You can use any type of fruit in the clafoutis.

MAKES 4–5 INDIVIDUAL CLAFOUTIS

Tray of claufoutis tarts in oven

Preparation of crispy orange tuile

CRISPY ORANGE TUILE, CHOCOLATE MOUSSE AND SZECHUAN PEPPER ICE-CREAM

The candied tomatoes will be the subject of some lively discussion among your guests, as well as the spicy chilli pepper flavour of the Szechuan pepper ice-cream, which perfectly compliments the chocolate and orange.

ORANGE TUILE

100g (3½ oz) sugar

50g (1¾ oz) butter, melted

25g (¾ oz) flour

zest of 1 orange

75g (2½ oz) almond flakes, extra finely chopped

50ml (1¾ fl oz) orange juice

CHOCOLATE MOUSSE

3 egg yolks

20g (²/₃ oz) sugar

150ml (5¼ fl oz) milk

75ml (2½ fl oz) cream

1 gelatine sheet, soaked in cold water

100g (3½ oz) milk chocolate

30g (1 oz) dark chocolate (70%)

ORANGE TUILE

Preheat oven to 140°C (300°F, Gas Mark 2). In a bowl, whisk together sugar and melted butter. Add flour, orange zest, almond flakes and orange juice, mix well. Spread thinly onto plastic baking sheet in a 8cm x 4cm (3¼ in x 1½ in) rectangle shape and bake until golden. Remove and, while still hot, mould into a cylinder shape, using a small rolling pin or small bottle.

CHOCOLATE MOUSSE

In a bowl, whisk yolks with sugar to make a thick sabayon. In a saucepan, bring milk and cream to the boil and pour into the sabayon. Place mix back in saucepan on low heat and continue to cook slowly until it thickens, do not boil.

Remove gelatin from cold water and squeeze out excess water. Whisk gelatine into custard mix. Cool to room temperature. In a double boiler or microwave, melt chocolate, and allow to cool to room temperature. When the two mixes are the same temperature, fold them together. Allow to set in fridge. Once set, whisk mousse and spoon into a piping bag. Set aside.

CANDIED TOMATOES

50ml (1¾ fl oz) sugar syrup (see Pantry)
1 vanilla bean
1 punnet roma cherry tomatoes, halved

CANDIED TOMATOES

Preheat oven to 50°C–60°C (125°F–140°F, Gas Mark 1). In a small saucepan, place the sugar syrup and vanilla bean and warm slightly for 5 minutes to infuse. Strain.

Place tomatoes, cut side up on a tray lined with baking paper and bake in the oven on very low heat until dry and chewy but not hard.

SERVING

On serving plates, place orange tuile upright and slightly off-centre. Fill $1/3$ of the tuile with the chocolate mousse. Place 3 pieces of candied tomato on top and fill another $1/3$ of the tuile, balancing a quenelle of Szechuan ice-cream on top. (See Ice-creams & Sorbets.)

SERVES 4–6

Crispy orange tuile, chocolate mousse and Szechuan pepper ice-cream

CARAMELISED PINEAPPLE, GINGER CREAM AND LEMON MYRTLE ICE-CREAM

This dessert is a progressive adventure in intensity, starting with the pineapple and then increasing with the spices, the ginger cream and then finally the lemon myrtle. The crumble adds the textural element.

POACHED PINEAPPLE

½ pineapple, skin removed
500ml (16 fl oz) light sugar syrup
  (see Pantry)
½ vanilla bean
1 cinnamon stick
1 clove
1 star-anise
3 cardamom pods

GINGER CREAM

250ml (8 fl oz) cream
1 tablespoon ginger, peeled and grated
4 egg yolks
85g (3 oz) sugar
1½ gelatine sheets, soaked

POACHED PINEAPPLE

In a saucepan, simmer all the ingredients for 1 hour. Remove from heat and let pineapple cool in liquid. Once cool, remove the pineapple and place onto a paper towel to absorb any excess liquid. Cut into small triangles.

GINGER CREAM

In a saucepan, bring cream to the boil, add the ginger, remove from the heat and leave to infuse for 5 minutes. Meanwhile, cream yolks and sugar in a bowl. Strain and pour the cream over the sugar and yolk mixture. In a saucepan, cook mixture into the consistency of an anglaise and remove from the heat. Add the gelatine and set in the fridge. Once set, whip in the ginger cream and place into a bowl until needed.

SABLE CRUMBLE

150g (5 oz) butter

50g (1¾ oz) sugar

zest of ¼ lemon

25g (½) egg

165g (5½ oz) plain/all purpose flour

60g (2 oz) almond meal

60g (2 oz) icing sugar

SABLE CRUMBLE

Cream butter and sugar until pale. Add the lemon zest, egg, flour, almond meal and icing sugar. When combined, rest the dough for 1 hour.

Preheat oven to 160°C (325°F, Gas Mark 2–3). Roll mixture out until 5mm (¼ in) thick. Place on a baking tray lined with baking paper and bake for 8–10 minutes or until golden brown. Cool and then crumble into small pieces.

TO ASSEMBLE

Place a piece of pineapple onto a tray, sprinkle with sugar and caramelise with a blow torch or under grill. Place on the plate. Make a line with the sable crumble and place a small quenelle of ginger cream at one end and a line of lemon myrtle ice-cream on the other end.

NOTE: We find Bethonga pineapples from Queensland, Australia, best for this recipe. They are the best quality for poaching and already have a natural, mildly spiced flavour.

SERVES 6–8

JASMINETEACREAM BRÛLÉEWITHSPICED LYCHEES

JASMINE TEA BRÛLÉE

100ml (3½ fl oz) milk

220ml (7⅞ fl oz) cream

1 tablespoon Chinese jasmine tea

6 egg yolks

70g (2⅓ oz) caster sugar

¼ vanilla bean

SPICED LYCHEES

zest of ½ lemon

zest of ½ lime

200ml (7 fl oz) sugar syrup

¼ vanilla bean

pinch white peppercorns (cracked)

1 small dried chilli

1 sprig coriander/cilantro with root,
   washed well

1 sprig mint, leaves only

200g (2½ oz) fresh lychees (skin and
   seed removed)

JASMINE TEA BRÛLÉE

Bring the milk and cream to the boil and infuse the tea. Whisk the yolks and sugar and pour over the strained milk and cream. Place the mix into a small container for a few hours or let rest overnight. The following day, let the mix come to room temperature and skim off any residue. Fill the brûlée moulds ¾ full with the mixture and bake in a fan-forced oven at 120°C (250°F, Gas Mark 1) or in a standard oven at 140°C (300°F, Gas Mark 2) for 15–20 minutes. The brûlée should have a slight wobble. Place in refridgerator until cold.

When ready to serve, sprinkle a good layer of caster sugar over the brûlée and use a blowtorch to caramelise.

SPICED LYCHEES

Bring the sugar syrup to the boil and infuse with the spices and herbs until cool. Strain and pour over the lychees. Leave in the fridge overnight so the flavour will intensify.

NOTE: The brûlée mix can be made the day before.

The best way to caramelise a crème brûlée is by using a small blowtorch, which is a very useful and relatively inexpensive piece of equipment.

Lychees are the best fruits to go with tea, especially jasmine tea. Logans or rambutans can be substituted for lychees.

SERVES 4

GINGERBREAD PUDDING WITH SAUCE SUZETTE

In this pudding recipe, we have replaced flour with gingerbread cake to give it more flavour and, more importantly, a much lighter texture. If you have some gingerbread cake left over you can freeze it and reuse it when needed. Be generous with the sauce suzette and you will see it is a heresy to serve ice-cream with this hot pudding—it is so good by itself.

GINGERBREAD CAKE

100g (3½ oz) plain/all purpose flour

1 teaspoon ground ginger

½ teaspoon mixed spice

½ teaspoon bicarbonate of soda

50g (1²/₃ oz) soft brown sugar

50g (1²/₃ oz) butter

3 tablespoons treacle

2 tablespoons golden syrup

75ml (2½ fl oz) milk

1 egg

GINGER PUDDING MIX

100g (3½ oz) butter

50g (1²/₃ oz) sugar

80g (2²/₃ oz) praline paste

3 tablespoons candied fruits, diced small
  (pear, pineapple, apricot)

200g (6½ oz) gingerbread cake,
  crumbled

25g (¾ oz) plain/all purpose flour

5 egg yolks

GINGERBREAD CAKE

Preheat oven to 130°C (250°F, Gas Mark 1). Sieve the flour, ginger, spice and bicarbonate of soda together. Add the brown sugar.

Melt the butter and dissolve the treacle and golden syrup in it. Once the butter mix is cool, add the milk, egg and the dry ingredients. Pour the mixture into a shallow baking tin and bake for 20 minutes or until spongy.

When cooled, crumble the cake in your hands to use in the pudding.

PUDDING

Preheat oven 180°C (350°F, Gas Mark 4). Cream butter and sugar. Add praline paste, candied fruits, gingerbread cake and flour. Blanch the yolks with the brown sugar, add the golden syrup and treacle and whisk until light and fluffy. Using a strong whisk, combine the two mixtures together. Whisk the eggwhites with the cream of tartar and the sugar until you have stiff peaks. Fold through the cake mix and place into small round metal moulds which have been buttered. Bake for 10 minutes, or until cooked.

40g (1 1/3 oz) soft brown sugar
1 tablespoon golden syrup
1 tablespoon treacle
75ml eggwhite
1/4 teaspoon cream of tartar
2 teaspoons sugar

SAUCE SUZETTE
150g (5 oz) sugar
250ml (8 fl oz) orange juice
20g (2/3 oz) butter

SAUCE SUZETTE
Make a dry caramel with the sugar and deglaze with the orange juice. Reduce to coating consistency. To serve, whisk in some butter and pour over the ginger pudding.

SERVES 4–6

Gingerbread pudding with sauce suzette

GINGE
PUDDI
WITHS
SUZETT

PEAR AND WALNUT TART WITH A CREAM GLAZE

This tart is a favourite with the restaurant staff and our pastry chef, Romina, has excelled with this dish. She has had to teach everyone how to make it so they can then prepare it for their families on their day off. If your staff ask you for a recipe for their family, you know you are making people very happy.

SWEET PASTRY
300g (10 oz) soft butter
300g (10 oz) caster sugar
pinch salt
2 eggs
450g (15 oz) plain/all purpose flour, sifted

CREAM FRANGIPANE
150g (5 oz) almond meal
150g (5 oz) sugar
150g (5oz) butter
3 eggs

SWEET PASTRY
In a kitchen mixer with a paddle, cream the butter, sugar and salt until pale. Add the eggs and flour and combine. Remove pastry from the kitchen mixer and place in the fridge to set for at least 1 hour. Roll the pastry out to 5mm (¼ in) thick and place in a tart baking tin. Trim the sides and blind bake in the oven until golden.

NOTE: You will have excess pastry, however, you can freeze what is not required and use at a later date.

CREAM FRANGIPANE
Stir the almond meal and sugar together. In a separate bowl, mix the butter until soft and stir in the eggs, sugar and almond meal.

GLAZE

5 yolks

100ml (3½ fl oz) cream

1 tablespoon sugar

POACHED PEARS

4 beurre bosc pears, peeled, halved and core removed

400ml (12½ fl oz) sugar syrup (see Pantry)

1 star-anise

3 cardamom pods

½ cinnamon stick

½ vanilla bean

GLAZE

Place all ingredients in a bowl. Mix together and set aside.

POACHED PEARS

In a saucepan, poach the pears in the sugar syrup with the spices until tender. Remove from pan and leave to cool. Once cool, slice the pears and fan slightly.

Preheat oven to 160°C (325°F, Gas Mark 2–3). Once the pastry has cooled, place half of the frangipane mix on the bottom of the tart dish and place the pears on top. Sprinkle with some fresh roasted walnuts and place some more frangipane on top so it comes ¾ of the way up the pastry. Bake in the oven for 20 minutes, then apply glaze and cook for a further 15–20 minutes.

NOTE: Pastry, poached pear and cream frangipane can all be prepared a few days before using.

MAKES 1 TART THAT SERVES 6–8

Pear and walnut tart with a cream glaze

CHOCOLATE SOUFFLÉ WITH SPICED CHOCOLATE ICE-CREAM

CHOCOLATE SOUFFLÉ

3 egg yolks

15g (½ oz) cornflour/cornstarch

125ml (4 fl oz) milk

90g (3 oz) chocolate (70% cocoa)

1 teaspoon cocoa

125ml (4 fl oz) eggwhite (about 4 x 30g eggs)

70g (2⅓ oz) sugar

knob of butter

sprinkle of sugar

icing sugar, to dust

Preheat oven to 170°C (325°F, Gas Mark 2–3). In a bowl, whisk the egg yolks and stir in the cornflour/cornstarch.

In a saucepan, bring milk to the boil and pour over the egg mixture. Place back into the pan and whisk over a medium heat until it thickens and continue cooking for a further 30 seconds. Remove from the heat.

In a double boiler or microwave, melt chocolate and mix in cocoa. Add to milk and egg mixture and let cool to room temperature.

Whisk the eggwhite with the sugar until medium peaks form and it is shiny. Fold into the chocolate mix and place into buttered moulds which have been dusted with sugar. Bake for about 7–8 minutes. Once cooked, dust with icing sugar and serve with spiced chocolate ice-cream (see Ice-creams & Sorbets).

SERVES 6

RASPBERRY BAVAROIS WITH COCONUT SORBET AND ALMOND TUILE

A very light mousse incorporating the unique cooking technique of Italian meringue. It is very simple and quick to make and can be made to any shape and size. The tuile can be curved or flat to cover the bavarois and you can garnish with any type of fruits. The raspberry flavour will accommodate a variety of flavours, and the coconut sorbet works very well with any tropical fruit you care to use as a garnish.

RASPBERRY BASE

200ml (7 fl oz) raspberry coulis
2 egg yolks
35g (1½ oz) sugar
2 gelatine leaves

ITALIAN MERINGUE

100g (3½ oz) sugar
75ml (2½ fl oz) eggwhite,
   approximately
   3 x 25g (1oz) eggs)
120ml (4 fl oz) cream, whipped to
   medium peaks

ALMOND TUILE

60g (2 oz) sugar
13g (³/₈ oz) flour
15g (½ oz) butter, melted
50g eggwhite (approximately 2 x
   25g/1oz eggs)
75g (2½ oz) flaked almonds, toasted

RASPBERRY BASE

Heat the coulis and pour over the blanched yolks and sugar. Place back onto the heat and cook as per the anglaise recipe, (see Caramelised Pineapple, Ginger Cream, and Lemon Myrtle Ice-cream). Remove from the heat and add the gelatine.

ITALIAN MERINGUE

To make the meringue, heat sugar and a small amount of water in a pot. As the sugar reaches 110°C–114°C (225°F–235°F), start to whip eggwhites. As the sugar reaches 118°C (245°F), pour the eggwhites over in a slow, steady stream while still whisking. Cool.

When cool, fold through the raspberry base then fold through the whipped cream. Place into a piping bag and pipe into 5cm (2 in) high ring moulds and allow to set overnight. Remove by sliding a warm knife around the sides of the mould.

ALMOND TUILE

Preheat oven to 120°C (250°F, Gas Mark 1). Mix all ingredients together except the almonds. Fold through the almonds and spread thin 6cm (2¹/₃ in) rounds onto a silpat. Bake in oven until golden. Remove from silpat and place over a rolling pin to make a half circle shape.

For Coconut Sorbet, see Ice Creams & Sorbets.

To serve, serve on a bed of rasberry base with the meringue and tuile on the side.

SERVES 4–6

Ice-
creams
Sorbets

COCONUTSORBET

Nothing is more magical than freshly made ice-cream and sorbet. In the restaurant, when the pastry section starts to churn the ice-cream and sorbet, it immediately becomes the busiest and most crowded section of the kitchen as everybody rushes in to have a taste.

At home, when my daughter Joanna makes her own ice-cream, there are always plenty of people offering to help clean the machine afterwards.

220ml (7½ fl oz) sugar syrup (see Pantry)
40g (1⅓ oz) trimoline (see Pantry)
500ml (16 fl oz) coconut milk
100ml (3½ fl oz) cream
juice of ½ a lime

Heat the sugar syrup in a saucepan. Add the trimoline and stir to dissolve. Mix it into the other ingredients and cool. Churn in an ice-cream machine.

FEIJOAAND LIMESORBET

1.5 kg (3lb) feijoas (see Pantry), peeled

100g sugar

330ml sugar syrup (see Pantry)

1 tablespoon trimoline (see Pantry)

1 knob ginger

¼ bunch mint

1 tablespoon roasted Szechuan pepper
  (see Pantry)

4 kaffir lime leaves (see Pantry)

20ml (¾ oz) lime juice, plus zest

handful stinging nettles, blanched

In a saucepan, cook feijoas with sugar until they are soft. Place into a blender, then pass through a fine strainer, reserving the juice.

Warm sugar syrup in a saucepan. Add the trimoline and stir to dissolve. Place ginger, mint, Szechuan pepper, kaffir lime leaves, lime juice and zest into syrup to infuse for 5–10 minutes. Strain syrup into feijoa puree.

Puree stinging nettles with some water. Strain and add to sorbet mix for colour and to intensify the natural peppery flavour of the feijoa. Stinging nettles have a natural pepper and salt flavour—perhaps this is why they are the favourite food of the snail—marvellous little gastronomes!

SPICEDCHOCOLATE ICE-CREAM

Using chilli for this recipe is inspired by the Incas, who were absolute experts in chocolate and used it in many different ways, particularly with spices. The intense flavour of the chocolate remains on your pallet for a long time with the help of the mild chilli influence.

200g (6½ oz) sugar

150ml water

8 yolks

300ml (10½ fl oz) milk

400ml (14 fl oz) cream

2 red birdseye chillies, sliced, seeds in

100g (3½ oz) dark chocolate, 70% cocoa

1 tablespoon cocoa powder

Make sabayon by heating sugar and water to 118°C (244°F)—use a sugar themometer to get an accurate temperature. Pour the egg yolks over the mixture and whisk until cool.

In a saucepan, bring milk and cream to boil and infuse with the chilli. Strain and add the chocolate and cocoa. Allow to cool. Mix with the sabayon and churn in an ice-cream machine.

OLIVEOIL ICE-CREAM

We developed this ice-cream from the subtle flavours of the first pressed olives. It has a subtle Mediterranean flavour which can be incorporated between 2 sheets of crispy parmesan as a lovely accompaniment for a matured semi-hard cheese.

250ml (8 fl oz) milk
50ml (1¾ fl oz) cream
20g (²/₃ oz) milk powder
½ vanilla pod
½ tablespoon trimoline (see Pantry)
5 egg yolks
125g (4 oz) sugar
120g (3¾ oz) olive oil

In a saucepan, bring milk, cream, milk powder, vanilla and trimoline to the boil. Whisk yolks with sugar until pale. Pour milk mixture over. Put back on stove and cook into an anglaise. Remove from the heat and cool to room temperature. Add the olive oil gradually to taste. Once cool, churn in an ice-cream machine.

LEMONMYRTLEAND BUSHPEPPERBERRY ICE-CREAM

200g (7oz) sugar

8 yolks

300ml (10½ fl oz) milk

400ml (12½ fl oz) cream

2 teaspoons (21g) of dried lemon myrtle (see Pantry)

1 teaspoon dried bush pepper berry (see Pantry)

Make sabayon by heating sugar and water to 118°C (244°F)—use a sugar themometer to get an accurate temperature. Pour the egg yolks over the mixture and whisk until cool.

In a saucepan, bring milk and cream to boil and infuse with lemon myrtle and bush pepper berry. After 10 mintues, strain milk mix and mix with sabayon. Allow to cool and churn in an ice-cream machine.

SZECHUAN PEPPER ICE-CREAM

200g (6½ oz) sugar
8 yolks
300ml (10½ fl oz) milk
400ml (12½ fl oz) cream
1½ tablespoons Szechuan pepper

Make sabayon by heating sugar and water to 118°C (244°F)—use a sugar themometer to get an accurate temperature. Pour the egg yolks over the mixture and whisk until cool.

Bring milk and cream to boil and infuse with pepper. Strain after 10 minutes and mix with sabayon. Once cool, churn in an ice-cream machine.

MANGO AND PASSIONFRUIT SORBET

4 mangoes, peeled and deseeded

750ml (24 fl oz) light sugar syrup (see Pantry)

3 passionfruit

330g (11 fl oz) sugar syrup

1 tablespoon trimoline (see Pantry)

Poach the mangoes in the sugar syrup until they are soft. Remove from the liquid and puree. Add passionfruit, including seeds.

Warm the sugar syrup and whisk in the trimoline until it is dissolved. Add to the puree and churn in an ice-cream machine.

MAKES 1KG (2LB)

Cibes

CHICKENSTOCK

2kg (4 lb) chicken bones, cleaned of any fat
1 carrot, thickly sliced
1 celery stick, thickly sliced
1 onion, cut in quarters
½ head garlic
bouquet garni (see Pantry)
water to cover

Put all of the ingredients in a saucepan or stock pot, vegetables on the bottom, bones on top, and cover with cold water. Cook on low heat and bring to a simmer (don't allow to boil, this will produce a cloudy stock). Simmer for 4 hours, be sure to skim your stock of fats and floating particles frequently, and then pass through a fine strainer and muslin cloth. If you are not using it straightaway, allow to cool slightly then refrigerate.

MAKES 2L (64 FL OZ)

DASHI STOCK

500ml (16 fl oz) water

1 piece kombu, 3cm x 5cm (1¼ in x 2 in)
  (see Pantry)

10g (⅓ oz) bonito flakes (see Pantry)

Place water and kombu in a medium saucepan and bring up to 75°C (150°F) or until small bubbles just start to appear on the bottom of the pan. Remove from heat and allow to cool for 10 minutes. Return to heat and bring back to 75°C (150°F), remove from heat and add bonito. Allow to steep for 10 minutes and then pass through a fine sieve.

MAKES 500ML (16 FL OZ)

VEGETABLESTOCK

1 carrot, finely sliced

2 celery sticks, finely sliced

1 brown onion, finely sliced

3 cloves garlic, finely sliced

1 teaspoon black peppercorns

2 sprigs thyme

1 bay leaf

Place all ingredients in a saucepan and cover with cold water. Bring to a simmer and cook for 15–20 minutes. Pass through a fine sieve then muslin cloth and allow to cool.

MAKES 1L (32 FL OZ)

MASTERSTOCK

4L (128 fl oz) water

300ml (10½ fl oz) shaoxing wine (see Pantry)

250ml (8 fl oz) light soy sauce

350ml (11½ fl oz) kecap manis (see Pantry)

1 tablespoon fennel seeds

1 tablespoon cardamom pods

2 teaspoons Szechuan pepper (see Pantry)

5 chillies, deseeded

2 tablespoons sliced ginger

6 star-anise

2 sticks cassia bark (see Pantry)

zest of 2 oranges

150g (5 oz) palm sugar

In a large saucepan, bring all ingredients to the boil and simmer for 1 hour.

You will require this quantity of masterstock for the whole tea-smoked chicken, or halve or even quarter this recipe to suit your requirements.

MAKES 5L (160 FL OZ)

CRISPYPARMESANTUILE

200g (6½ oz) parmesan, finely grated
1 teaspoon plain/all purpose flour

Mix the parmesan and flour together in a bowl. Heat a medium frying pan on low heat, sprinkle in the cheese mixture in a thin layer and cook until golden brown, then flip and lightly brown the other side.

SERVES 4

CRUSTACEAN**BASE**

½ onion, diced

½ carrot, diced

1 celery stick, diced

2 garlic cloves

2 tablespoons olive oil

400g (13 oz) crustacean shells, cleaned,
  such as prawn, crayfish, crab etc.

1 tablespoon tomato paste

2 ripe tomatoes

salt and cayenne pepper

25ml (⁷/₈ fl oz) brandy

120ml (4 fl oz) white wine

In a saucepan, sauté onion, carrot, celery and garlic with a small amount of oil. Meanwhile, in a separate pan, fry crustacean shells. When the vegetables start to colour, add tomato paste and fry gently for a minute or two, add the shells to your vegetables, then the tomatoes and season with salt and cayenne pepper. Add brandy and flame to burn off the alcohol, then add the white wine and cover ¾ the way up the shells with water. Simmer for 20 minutes, then pass through a fine sieve.

MAKES 50ML (2 FL OZ)

TEMPURABATTER

½ cup plain/all purpose flour
¼ cup of cornflour/cornstarch
1½ teaspoons baking powder
130–160ml soda water, icy cold

Combine flour, cornflour/cornstarch and baking powder. Add soda water, folding together to form a thin batter. Do not work too much as you need it to appear lumpy to be nice and crispy when cooked.

SERVES 4–8

BRIKPASTRY

3 tablespoons clarified butter (see
  Pantry), melted
2 sheets brik or filo pastry
zest of 1 lemon

Lay out 1 sheet of pastry, lightly butter and sprinkle with lemon zest. Lay the other sheet of pastry on top and press together well. Brush top pastry layer with clarified butter. Cut the pastry into 2.5cm x 5cm (1 in x 2 in) lengths.

Layer between baking paper and put a tray on top to keep pastry flat. Cook at 170°C (325°F, Gas Mark 4) for 9 minutes or until golden and crispy.

SERVES 4

TTE PEPPER

GROUND NUTMEG

RD SEEDS

GROUND CINAMON

PIN

WDER

BLACK SESAME

C

MACADAMIA'S

EDS.

DRIED CRANBERRIES

ki

In the
tchen

PANTRY

We recommend you include a few of the Asian ingredients below in your pantry. You don't need large quantities of each ingredient, but they do appear in quite a few different recipes and have a long shelf life.

ASAFOETIDA

A plant from the Apiaceae family, which includes carrots, parsley, dill, celery, caraway and fennel. Similar in appearance to fennel, it is used mainly in Indian cuisine.

BETEL LEAVES

The leaves of a palm grown and cultivated in most of south and South-East Asia and used in cooking to wrap, store, smoke and simmer food.

BONITO FLAKES

A crucial fish ingredient in Japanese cuisine and a fundamental component of many stocks and sauces. It is readily available in Asian markets in the form of flakes or pellets designed to be dissolved in water or rice wine.

BOUQUET GARNI

A small bunch of fresh herbs and spices tied together using string and cheese/muslin cloth and used to flavour soups, stocks, sauces and casseroles.

BUSH PEPPER BERRY

The dried berry of a Tasmanian plant of the Winteraceae family, used in Australian cooking for marinades, grilled meats and stews. While not the same flavour, Tasmanian pepper berries share some of the attributes of Szechuan pepper.

CANDLENUT

A creamy coloured round nut, often used in Indonesian and Malaysian cooking. Macadamia nuts can be used as a substitute, but the candlenut has a more bitter taste.

CASSIA BARK

The outer layer of bark of the cassia tree, native to China. Similar to cinnamon sticks but with a stronger flavour and dark red-brown colour.

CAVALO NERO

Also known as black cabbage, it is a loose-leaf cabbage from Italy, with long, dark green leaves and a pleasantly tangy, bitter flavour with a sweet aftertaste.

CHINESE BLACK VINEGAR

Vinegar made from rice or wheat and allowed to oxidise and ferment. Sugar, spices and caramel colouring can be added. Similar to balsamic vinegar, it is used in Chinese stir-frys, braises and sauces.

CHINESE RICE WINE

Wine made from fermented glutinous rice. Usually served warm as a drink, but used in cooking in sauces and marinades. Dry sherry can be substituted.

CITRUS PONZU

The juice of the Japanese citrus fruit yuzu or citron. Lemon, lime or grapefruit can be substituted.

CLARIFIED BUTTER

Known as ghee in Indian cuisine, clarified butter is pure butter fat. It is readily available in supermarkets but is easily made by melting butter and scooping the liquid from the milk solids that form on the bottom of the pan.

CREPINETTE

The fatty membrane that surrounds internal organs of some animals such as cows, sheep and pigs. It is often used as a natural sausage casing. It is often used as a natural sausage: think of it as nature's cling wrap. Available at butchers or gourmet delis.

DAIKON

A white radish, shaped like a large carrot, used extensively in Japanese cooking. It has a crisp juicy flesh and mild, refreshing taste. It can be grated, shredded, pickled or sliced.

FEIJOAS

An aromatic, oval fruit with a thin, waxy, green skin and creamy coloured flesh. It is closely related to the guava.

FISH SAUCE

A sauce made from the liquid of salted fish allowed to ferment.

FLOSSY SALT

A refined grain of salt that is used for cooking and curing.

GALANGAL

A root-like stem closely related to ginger, but milder in flavour.

GRIBICHE

An egg dressing or mayonnaise made from hard-boiled eggs and mustard. Chives, red onion, capers, parsley, chervil and tarragon can also be added.

HIJIKI
Dried seaweed with a strong fish taste, filled with essential vitamins and minerals.

HOISIN SAUCE
A sweet, spicy, salty soybean-based sauce made with garlic, chilli and vinegar.

KAFFIR LIME LEAVES
From the South-East Asian citrus tree, kaffir, the leaves are very fragrant and common in Asian cuisine.

KAISERFLEISCH
Italian smoked pork belly, similar to speck, smoky bacon can be substituted.

KECAP MANIS
A sweet sauce Kecap made by fermenting soybeans with salt and other ingredients. There are two major types of Indonesian soy sauce—kecap manis and kecap asin. Both are available from Asian supermarkets.

KIRSCH
A liqueur distilled from cherries, widely used as a flavouring in pastries and desserts.

KOHLRABI
a cultivated variety of cabbage. The flesh has a turnip-like flavour.

KOMBU
A type of edible seaweed important in Japanese cuisine. It can be found fresh, dried, pickled, and frozen in many Asian markets and supermarkets.

LECITHIN
A fatty acid or lipid-based compound naturally occurring in animal and plant tissue and in egg yolk. It is used as an emulsifier to create surface tension and suspend liquids, such as bubbles in sauces, longer.

LEMON MYRTLE
Also known as lemon-scented myrtle, it is a flowering plant native to Queensland, Australia. The leaves are used to produce essential oil or tea. In cooking, whole or dried ground lemon myrtle leaves are used in marinades, poultry and rice dishes.

LILLY PILLY CAPERS
Also known as riberries, they are small, red, pear-shaped fruits from Australian native rainforest trees with a pleasant, spicy flavour. Available from supermarkets.

MICRO HERBS

Baby herbs harvested in the first stage of growth, typically 10–25 days. Though small in size they are intensely flavored and beautiful.

MIRIN

Sweet-tasting, low alcohol rice wine from Japan. In cooking it adds a dash of sweetness to dishes and sauces. It is sometimes employed as a ceremonial drink at the beginning of the New Year and a few other special occasions.

MISO

Fermented paste of soya beans used in soups, sauces, dressings and to season meat or fish. Varies in variety from the strong-tasting red to the mild-tasting white.

NUOC NAM

A chilli-based sauce made from fish with salty, sour, spicy and sweet flavours.

PANDAN LEAVES

Long, stiff, bright green leaves from the pandanus tree with a distinctive sweet, nutty flavour. The young leaves are used to add flavour and colour to food during cooking.

PANKO

Japanese breadcrumbs, they are lighter, crispier and crunchier than regular breadcrumbs. Available from Asian specialty stores and large supermarkets.

QUINOA

Pronouced KEEN-wah. A small grain native to South America. It is low in fat and carbohydrates. Available from health food stores and large supermarkets, it is boiled and served like rice.

RED DRAGON FRUIT

A beautiful looking and tasting fruit thought to have come from South America. The flesh comes in two main colours; red with black seeds and white with black seeds, with a sweet tasting pulp.

RED MISO PASTE

See Miso

RICE VINEGAR AND RICE WINE VINEGAR

Fermented rice vinegar, slightly sweet and nearly colourless. Rice wine vinegar is made from sake and is a variant on the 'wine' vinegar most people are familiar with. Often called seasoned rice vinegar, it exhibits a stronger taste. It is also a common ingredient in sushi.

SANCHO

The dried bud of the flower from a Japanese pepper tree, similar to peppercorns.

SHAO XING WINE

A traditional Chinese fermented wine made from rice, aged for 10 or more years and used for cooking and drinking.

SHIITAKE

A Japanese mushroom, dried or fresh, with a strong meaty and earthy flavour. Can be found in most supermarkets.

SHISO

A Japanese herb, part of the mint family. Can be found in Japanese specialty stores or Asian food stores.

SUGAR SYRUP

Also known as simple syrup, bar syrup or simple sugar syrup, it is a very basic combination of one part sugar to one part water. Bring the water to boil in a pan and then add the sugar, stirring until the sugar dissolves completely. Remove from the heat and allowed to cool completely. Light sugar syrup has 15 per cent less sugar and more water.

SZECHUAN PEPPER

Dried berries from the Chinese prickly ash tree with a sharp and spicy flavour and one of the components of five-spice powder.

TAMARIND

The pulp of the fruit from the tamarind tree used in Asian cuisine to add sourness. Often sold dried it needs to be soaked in hot water, squeezed and strained before use.

TOGARASHI

A Japanese seven-spice blend that typically includes red chilli flakes, dried orange peel, white sesame seeds, black sesame seeds, nori (seaweed) flakes, poppy seeds and ginger.

TRIMOLINE

Inverted sugar liquid that helps ice-cream and sorbet stay smooth. It can be made by bringing a mixture of two parts (by weight) granulated sucrose and one part water to a boil and then reduce the heat to a low simmer for five to seven minutes until the solution becomes clear.

TRUFFLE JUICE/TRUFFLE OIL

Truffle juice or oil is flavoured by steeping and pressing truffles to extract the liquid or as a by-product of the truffle canning process and is simply the liquid that accompanies truffles in their can or jar. They are available from specialty grocery stores.

VERJUICE

An acidic juice made from unfermented grapes. Used in place of vinegar, it can be flavoured with ingredients such as sorrel or lemon.

WASABI

A Japanese root vegetable very similar to horseradish with a slightly more subtle flavour when used fresh. Best in paste form, the powdered form is a little hotter due to the use of horseradish.

WHITE MISO PASTE

See Miso

WINTER MELON

A large, round melon from east and South-East Asia and used in soups in the same way as daikon.

WOMBOK

Also known as Chinese cabbage, womboks have a sweet, mild flavour. While the leaf blades can be slightly peppery, the thick white ribs are sweet and juicy.

GLOSSARY

An explanation of cooking terms used throughout the book.

ANGLAISE

A dessert sauce made of cream and thickened with eggs and flavoured with vanilla or to cook food in water or white stock.

BEIGNET

A dough that may be used for sweet or savoury purposes with fillings of meat, seafood, potatoes, mushrooms and other vegetables. Also choux pastry cooked like fritters.

BLANCH

A cooking process to enhance the colour, flavour and texture of ingredients. Blanching involves quickly cooking food in boiling water or a steamer and then plunging into cold water to stop the cooking process. Blanching is also the term given to mixing eggs or egg yolks with sugar as part of the process to start the cooking of an anglaise or similar.

BLIND BAKE

Baking a pastry shell without any filling. Baking paper is used to line the shell and a grain, like rice or even rock salt, is placed in it to weigh down the shell while baking to retain the shape.

BRUNOISE

The French cooking term given to cut into a very small, uniform dice.

CARAMELISE

To cook the natural sugars found in food. To caramelise sugar, heat a pan over medium heat and cover base with a light layer of sugar. The sugar will melt into a light brown syrup. Be careful of the heat as the sugar starts to colour.

CARTOUCHE

A round piece of silicon or baking paper used to cover the contents of a pan or casserole to help retain moisture during or after cooking. It can be used for keeping heat in while letting steam out. A cartouche can also be used to line a cake tin before baking.

CEVICHE

A dish of raw seafood dressed with a citrus-based sauce or dressing.

DEGLAZE

To add a small amount of liquid, such as wine or stock, to a pan to remove the sediment from cooking and used as a base for a sauce, gravy or to finish a gastric.

DOUBLE BOILER

A double-decker saucepan with an upper pot that fits into a lower pot. The bottom pot has boiling water and the ingredient is placed in the top pot and heated only by steam. Used to melt chocolate or other ingredients without burning or seizing or to cook delicate sauces such as beurre blanc.

EMULSION

Two or more ingredients mixed together using a whisk or mixer, such as egg yolks and olive oil in salad dressings or vinaigrettes, until they are suspended together and form a smooth and stable mixture.

FARCIE

The French cooking term for a filling or stuffing.

GASTRIC

A syrup or liquid made by creating caramel from sugar and deglazing with vinegar, a little at a time, to create a balance in flavour between sweet and sour.

INFUSE

to steep, soak or boil an ingredient in liquid to extract its flavour.

JULIENNE

To cut or slice ingredients into thin, even strips. This technique not only ensures that foods cook evenly and thoroughly, but also makes it look stylish on the plate.

LAMINATE

To roll pasta dough through a pasta machine until it appears to have a shine or gloss. This indicated that the pasta has been worked sufficiently and is ready to cook.

MANDOLINE

A slicer with sharp, adjustable blades to cuts fruit and vegetables into even and precise slices.

QUENELLE

Food molded into an oval egg shape such as a scoop of ice-cream or sorbet.

REDUCE

To boil a liquid to reduce its volume and concentrate its flavours.

SABAYON

The French term for whisking egg yolks and sugar until they are thick and fluffy.

SAUTÉ

To cook food in a shallow pan pan with a small amount of oil or fat and without coloring.

SILPAT

A non-stick silicon mat used in baking to provide a non-stick surface. Useful for making crystals and tuiles in pastry.

STEEPING

To soak an ingredient in hot or cold liquid for a period of time to soften or extract flavour.

SWEAT OFF

To cook an ingredient gently in oil or butter to soften them without colouring.

TEMPURA

A light crispy batter usually made from ice water or soda water.

RECIPE INDEX